Meals in a Jar

Effortless Recipes for Nutritious and Convenient Eating On-the-Go

by

Justeen Flynn

Table of Content

Introduction...**21**

Welcome to Meals in a Jar..21

Benefits of Jar Meals..21

1. Portability..22

2. Portion Control...22

3. Freshness..22

4. Eco-Friendly..22

5. Visual Appeal...22

6. Time-Saving...22

7. Versatility...23

8. Budget-Friendly..23

9. Healthier Eating Habits..23

10. Stress Reduction..23

How to Use This Book..23

1. Understanding the Structure..23

2. Recipe Layout...24

3. Icons and Symbols...24

4. Meal Prep and Storage Tips...24

5. Customizing Recipes..25

6. Exploring Advanced Techniques...25

7. Budgeting and Economizing...25

8.   25

Essential Tools and Ingredients..25

Essential Tools...25

1. Glass Jars..25

2. Measuring Cups and Spoons...26

3. Sharp Knives and Cutting Board..26

4. Mixing Bowls..26

5. Blender or Food Processor...26

6. Cooking Pots and Pans..26

7. Funnels..26

8. Spoons and Spatulas...26

Essential Ingredients..26

1. Grains and Pasta..2

2. Proteins...2

3. Fresh Vegetables...2

4. Fresh Fruits...2

5. Dairy and Dairy Alternatives..2

6. Nuts and Seeds...2

7. Oils and Vinegars..2

8. Herbs and Spices...2

9. Sweeteners...2

10. Miscellaneous..2

    Final Tips..2
    Chapter 1: Breakfast Jars 1.1..2
    Classic Overnight Oats 1.2..2
    Introduction..2
    Ingredients..2
    Instructions...2
    Tips and Variations..2
    Nutrition Information (Approximate per serving)..2
    Conclusion...2
    Berry Yogurt Parfait 1.3...3

Berry Yogurt Parfait 1.3..3
    Introduction..3
    Ingredients..3
    Preparation...3
    Tips and Variations..3
    Nutritional Information...3
    Conclusion...3
    Chia Seed Pudding Varieties 1.4..3
    Introduction..3
    Basic Chia Seed Pudding Recipe...3
    Chia Seed Pudding Varieties...3

1. Berry Bliss Pudding...3

2. Chocolate Chia Pudding...3

3. Tropical Coconut Chia Pudding...3

4. Matcha Green Tea Pudding...3

5. Apple Cinnamon Chia Pudding...33

Tips for Perfect Chia Seed Pudding...33

Nutritional Benefits...34

Conclusion...34

Smoothie Jars 1.5...34

Introduction...34

Basic Smoothie Jar Preparation...34

Smoothie Jar Recipes...35

1. Berry Green Smoothie...35

2. Tropical Sunrise Smoothie...35

3. Chocolate Peanut Butter Smoothie...35

4. Apple Cinnamon Smoothie...36

5. Avocado Mint Smoothie...36

Tips for Perfect Smoothie Jars...36

Nutritional Benefits...36

Conclusion...37

Nut Butter and Fruit Jars 1.6...37

Introduction...37

Basic Nut Butter and Fruit Jar Preparation...37

Nut Butter and Fruit Jar Recipes...37

1. Apple Almond Butter Delight...37

2. Banana Peanut Butter Bliss...38

3. Pear Cashew Butter Crunch...38

4. Berry Sunflower Seed Butter...38

5. Peach Almond Butter Fusion...39

Tips for Perfect Nut Butter and Fruit Jars...39

Nutritional Benefits...39

Conclusion...39

Savory Breakfast Jars...40

Introduction...40

Basic Savory Breakfast Jar Preparation...40

Savory Breakfast Jar Recipes...40

1. Southwest Quinoa Jar...40

2. Mediterranean Breakfast Jar...41

3. Hearty Breakfast Potatoes...41

4. Spinach and Feta Egg Jar..4

5. Breakfast Burrito Jar..4

Tips for Perfect Savory Breakfast Jars...4

Nutritional Benefits...4

Conclusion...4

Chapter 2:...4

Lunch Jars 2.1...4

Introduction...4

Basic Lunch Jar Preparation..4

Lunch Jar Recipes..4

1. Mediterranean Quinoa Jar..4

2. Asian Noodle Salad Jar...4

3. Southwest Chicken Jar..4

4. Greek Chicken Salad Jar..4

5. Roasted Veggie and Hummus Jar..4

Tips for Perfect Lunch Jars..4

Nutritional Benefits...4

Conclusion...4

Fresh Salads 2.2...4

Fresh Salads 2.2..**4**

Introduction...4

Basic Salad Jar Preparation..4

Fresh Salad Jar Recipes...4

1. Classic Caesar Salad Jar...4

2. Greek Salad Jar...4

3. Southwest Quinoa Salad Jar..4

4. Mediterranean Chickpea Salad Jar..4

5. Asian Noodle Salad Jar...4

Tips for Perfect Fresh Salad Jars...4

Nutritional Benefits...4

Conclusion...4

Hearty Grain Bowls 2.3..5

Introduction...5

Basic Hearty Grain Bowl Preparation..5

Hearty Grain Bowl Recipes..5

1. Mediterranean Farro Bowl..50

2. Asian-Inspired Rice Bowl..51

3. Southwest Quinoa Bowl..51

4. Roasted Veggie Barley Bowl..51

5. Greek Chicken and Rice Bowl..52

Tips for Perfect Hearty Grain Bowls..52

Nutritional Benefits..53

Conclusion..53

Protein-Packed Jars 2.4..53

Introduction..53

Basic Protein-Packed Jar Preparation..53

Protein-Packed Jar Recipes..54

1. Grilled Chicken and Quinoa Jar..54

2. Spicy Tofu and Sweet Potato Jar..54

3. Lentil and Veggie Jar..54

4. Turkey and Brown Rice Jar..55

5. Greek Yogurt and Chickpea Jar..55

Tips for Perfect Protein-Packed Jars..55

Nutritional Benefits..56

Conclusion..56

Vegetarian and Vegan Options 2.5..56

Introduction..56

Basic Vegetarian and Vegan Jar Preparation..56

Vegetarian and Vegan Jar Recipes..57

1. Mediterranean Chickpea Jar..57

2. Sweet Potato and Black Bean Jar..57

3. Vegan Lentil and Kale Jar..58

4. Thai Peanut Tofu Jar..58

5. Roasted Veggie and Hummus Jar..58

Tips for Perfect Vegetarian and Vegan Jars..59

Nutritional Benefits..59

Conclusion..59

International Flavors..59

Introduction..59

Basic International Jar Preparation..6

International Flavor Jar Recipes..6

1. Mexican Burrito Bowl Jar..6

2. Thai Peanut Noodle Jar...6

3. Greek Mezze Jar..6

4. Japanese Teriyaki Chicken Jar..6

5. Indian Chickpea Curry Jar..6

Tips for Perfect International Flavor Jars...6

Nutritional Benefits..6

Conclusion..6

Chapter 3:..6

Dinner Jars 3.1..6

Introduction...6

Basic Dinner Jar Preparation...6

Dinner Jar Recipes...6

1. Chicken and Veggie Stir-Fry Jar...

2. Beef and Sweet Potato Jar..

3. Vegetarian Chili Jar...

4. Thai Curry Tofu Jar...

5. Italian Pasta Jar..

Tips for Perfect Dinner Jars...6

Nutritional Benefits..6

Conclusion..

Comfort Food Jars 3.2..

Introduction...

Basic Comfort Food Jar Preparation..

Comfort Food Jar Recipes...

1. Classic Mac and Cheese Jar..

2. Beef Stroganoff Jar..

3. Chicken Pot Pie Jar..

4. Shepherd's Pie Jar...

5. Creamy Tomato Soup Jar...

Tips for Perfect Comfort Food Jars...

Nutritional Benefits..

Conclusion...69

Low-Carb and Keto Options 3.3..69

Introduction...69

Basic Low-Carb and Keto Jar Preparation..69

Low-Carb and Keto Jar Recipes..70

1. Chicken Caesar Salad Jar...70

2. Beef and Broccoli Stir-Fry Jar..70

3. Avocado and Egg Salad Jar...70

4. Salmon and Spinach Jar..71

5. Zucchini Noodles with Pesto Jar...71

Tips for Perfect Low-Carb and Keto Jars..71

Nutritional Benefits..72

Conclusion...72

One-Pot Meals 3.4..72

Introduction..72

Basic One-Pot Meal Jar Preparation..72

One-Pot Meal Jar Recipes...73

1. Chicken and Rice Soup Jar...73

2. Beef and Vegetable Stew Jar..73

3. Vegetarian Chili Jar...73

4. Shrimp and Quinoa Bowl Jar..74

5. Sausage and Pepper Pasta Jar..74

Tips for Perfect One-Pot Meal Jars...75

Nutritional Benefits..75

Conclusion...75

Family Favorites 3.5...75

Introduction..75

Basic Family Favorites Jar Preparation...75

Family Favorite Jar Recipes..76

1. Classic Meatloaf Jar...76

2. Creamy Chicken Alfredo Jar..76

3. Taco Night Jar..77

4. Spaghetti and Meatballs Jar...77

5. Cheesy Broccoli and Rice Casserole Jar..77

Tips for Perfect Family Favorite Jars..7

Nutritional Benefits...7

Conclusion..7

Gourmet in a Jar..7

Introduction...7

Basic Gourmet Jar Preparation...7

Gourmet Jar Recipes...7

1. Lobster and Truffle Risotto Jar..7

2. Duck Confit and Red Cabbage Jar...7

3. Salmon and Asparagus with Hollandaise Sauce Jar..8

4. Fig and Goat Cheese Salad Jar...8

5. Beef Wellington Jar...8

Tips for Perfect Gourmet Jars..8

Nutritional Benefits...8

Conclusion..8

Chapter 4:...8

Snack Jars 4.1...8

Introduction...8

Basic Snack Jar Preparation...8

Snack Jar Recipes...8

1. Veggie and Hummus Jar...8

2. Fruit and Yogurt Parfait Jar...8

3. Cheese and Crackers Jar...8

4. Nut and Dried Fruit Mix Jar..8

5. Apple Slices with Peanut Butter Jar..8

Tips for Perfect Snack Jars..8

Nutritional Benefits...8

Conclusion..8

Healthy Dips and Veggies 4.2..8

Introduction...8

Basic Healthy Dip and Veggie Jar Preparation...8

Healthy Dip and Veggie Jar Recipes...8

1. Classic Hummus and Veggies Jar...9

2. Creamy Avocado and Veggies Jar..9

3. Greek Yogurt Ranch Dip and Veggies Jar..9

4. Spicy Red Pepper Dip and Veggies Jar..86

5. Herbed Yogurt Dip and Veggies Jar..87

Tips for Perfect Healthy Dip and Veggie Jars...87

Nutritional Benefits..87

Conclusion...87

Fruit and Nut Mixes 4.3..88

Introduction...88

Basic Fruit and Nut Mix Preparation...88

Fruit and Nut Mix Recipes..88

1. Tropical Delight Mix..88

2. Berry Nut Crunch Mix...89

3. Classic Trail Mix...89

4. Nutty Apple Cinnamon Mix...89

5. Spiced Date and Nut Mix..90

Tips for Perfect Fruit and Nut Mixes..90

Nutritional Benefits..90

Conclusion...90

Protein Snacks 4.4..91

Introduction...91

Basic Protein Snack Jar Preparation...91

Protein Snack Jar Recipes..91

1. Greek Yogurt and Berry Bowl...91

2. Chicken Salad with Crackers..92

3. Tofu and Veggie Snack Jar...92

4. Cottage Cheese and Fruit Parfait..92

5. Hard-Boiled Eggs and Veggies...93

Tips for Perfect Protein Snack Jars...93

Nutritional Benefits..93

Conclusion...93

Quick Energy Boosters..94

Introduction...94

Basic Quick Energy Booster Jar Preparation...94

Quick Energy Booster Jar Recipes..94

1. Nut Butter and Banana Jar...94

2. Berry and Oat Energy Jar..95

3. Cottage Cheese and Fruit Energy Jar..9

4. Quick Protein-Packed Smoothie Jar..9

5. Energy Nut and Fruit Mix Jar..9

Tips for Perfect Quick Energy Boosters..9

Nutritional Benefits..9

Conclusion...9

Chapter 5:...9

Dessert Jars 5.1..9

Introduction...9

Basic Dessert Jar Preparation..9

Dessert Jar Recipes...9

1. Classic Chocolate Pudding Jar...9

2. Berry Yogurt Parfait...9

3. No-Bake Cheesecake Jar..9

4. Apple Cinnamon Oat Dessert Jar..9

5. Peach Cobbler in a Jar..9

Tips for Perfect Dessert Jars..9

Nutritional Benefits..9

Conclusion...9

Fruit-Based Desserts 5.2..9

Introduction...9

Basic Fruit-Based Dessert Jar Preparation..10

Fruit-Based Dessert Jar Recipes..10

1. Mango Coconut Chia Pudding..1

2. Berry Yogurt Crumble...1

3. Apple Cinnamon Delight..1

4. Peach Yogurt Parfait..1

5. Berry and Banana Oat Crumble...1

Tips for Perfect Fruit-Based Desserts..1

Nutritional Benefits..1

Conclusion...1

No-Bake Treats 5.4...1

Introduction...1

Basic No-Bake Treat Jar Preparation...1

No-Bake Treat Jar Recipes..1

1. Chocolate Peanut Butter Energy Balls...103

2. Coconut Almond Energy Bars..103

3. Berry Chia Seed Pudding...104

4. No-Bake Cheesecake Jars...104

5. Nut and Date Energy Bars...104

Tips for Perfect No-Bake Treats..105

Nutritional Benefits...105

Conclusion..105

Mini Cakes and Pies...105

Introduction..105

Basic Mini Cake and Pie Jar Preparation..105

Mini Cake and Pie Jar Recipes...106

1. Mini Chocolate Lava Cakes..106

2. Mini Apple Pies..106

3. Mini Lemon Cheesecakes..107

4. Mini Carrot Cake Jars..107

5. Mini Key Lime Pies...108

Tips for Perfect Mini Cakes and Pies..108

Nutritional Benefits...109

Conclusion..109

Chapter 6:...109

Kid-Friendly Jars 6.1...109

Introduction..109

Basic Kid-Friendly Jar Preparation...109

Kid-Friendly Jar Recipes..110

1. Fruit and Yogurt Parfait..110

2. Mini Pizza Jars...110

3. Rainbow Veggie and Hummus Jars..110

4. Nut Butter and Banana Oat Jars...111

5. DIY Trail Mix Jars...111

Tips for Perfect Kid-Friendly Jars..111

Nutritional Benefits...112

Conclusion..112

School Lunch Ideas 6.3...112

Introduction..11

Basic School Lunch Jar Preparation..11

School Lunch Jar Recipes..11

1. Chicken Caesar Salad Jars...11

2. Turkey and Cheese Roll-Up Jars...11

3. Quinoa and Veggie Power Bowl..11

4. Fruit and Yogurt Parfait..11

5. Pasta Salad Jars..11

6. Mini Sandwich Jars...11

Tips for Perfect School Lunch Jars...11

Nutritional Benefits...11

Conclusion..11

Chapter 7:..11

Fitness and Wellness Jars 7.1..11

Fitness and Wellness Jars 7.1..11

Introduction...11

Basic Fitness and Wellness Jar Preparation...11

Fitness and Wellness Jar Recipes...11

1. Protein-Packed Quinoa Salad...11

2. Greek Yogurt and Berry Smoothie Jars...11

3. Sweet Potato and Black Bean Power Bowl...11

4. Nut and Seed Energy Jars..1

5. Avocado and Egg Breakfast Jars..1

6. Chia Seed Pudding with Fresh Fruit...1

Tips for Perfect Fitness and Wellness Jars..11

Nutritional Benefits...11

Conclusion..11

High-Protein Meals 7.2..11

Introduction...11

Basic High-Protein Jar Preparation..12

High-Protein Jar Recipes..12

1. Chicken and Quinoa Power Bowl..1

2. Greek Yogurt and Berry Protein Parfait...1

3. Turkey and Veggie Stir-Fry Jars...1

4. Tofu and Vegetable Stir-Fry...1

5. Salmon and Avocado Rice Bowl..121

6. Cottage Cheese and Fruit Jar..122

Tips for Perfect High-Protein Jars..122

Nutritional Benefits..122

Conclusion..123

Post-Workout Snacks 7.3..123

Introduction..123

Basic Post-Workout Jar Preparation..123

Post-Workout Snack Jar Recipes..123

1. Greek Yogurt and Berry Recovery Jar..123

2. Cottage Cheese and Pineapple Bowl..124

3. Protein-Packed Smoothie Jar..124

4. Sweet Potato and Black Bean Snack..124

5. Chocolate Chia Seed Pudding..125

6. Almond Butter and Apple Slices..125

Tips for Perfect Post-Workout Jars..125

Nutritional Benefits..126

Conclusion..126

Detox Jars..126

Introduction..126

Basic Detox Jar Preparation..126

Detox Jar Recipes..127

1. Green Detox Smoothie Jar..127

2. Detox Veggie and Quinoa Salad..127

3. Berry and Chia Seed Detox Pudding..127

4. Turmeric and Avocado Detox Bowl..128

5. Cucumber and Mint Infused Water Jar..128

6. Sweet Potato and Kale Detox Bowl..129

Tips for Perfect Detox Jars..129

Nutritional Benefits..129

Conclusion..129

Conclusion..**130**

Embracing the Convenience..130

Nutritional Diversity and Balance..130

Practical Tips for Success..130

The Joy of Meal Prep...13
Looking Ahead...13

Bonus

Dear reader if you want a free ebook of these

1

2

3

4

5

6

write me "free copy" and
the number book you want
at ergabooks@gmail.com

Dear Reader, I hope this message finds you well. I am writing to kindly ask for your support. If you enjoyed reading my book, would you consider leaving a brief review? Your feedback is incredibly important to me and can significantly help other readers discover my work. Even a simple review can make a big difference. Thank you so much for your time and support!

Warm regards,

Justeen

Introduction

Welcome to Meals in a Jar

Welcome to the world of Meals in a Jar! If you're looking for a simple, delicious way to prepare your meals, you're in the right place. This book is designed for busy people who don't want to compromise on eating well. Every recipe you'll find here has been carefully selected and tested to ensure you get the most flavor and nutrition with the least effort.

Why Meals in a Jar? Our lives are busier than ever, and it can be challenging to find the time to prepare healthy, tasty meals every day. That's where jar meals come in. With just a few ingredients and a little bit of prep time, you can have meals ready to go for the entire week. They're perfect for work lunches, quick dinners, or even on-the-go snacks.

Meals in a jar are not just about convenience; they're about enjoying fresh, homemade food that you can feel good about. These recipes are designed to be easy to follow, using ingredients that are readily available and affordable. Whether you're a seasoned cook or a complete beginner, you'll find something here to love.

In this book, you'll discover a variety of recipes for every meal of the day—breakfast, lunch, dinner, snacks, and desserts. Each chapter is filled with ideas that are both practical and delicious, ensuring you never get bored with your meal options. Plus, we've included tips on meal prep, storage, and customization, so you can make each recipe your own.

Here's what you can expect from "Meals in a Jar Cookbook":

- **Simple and Tasty Recipes:** From classic overnight oats to gourmet dinner jars, every recipe is easy to make and full of flavor.
- **Healthy and Nutritious:** Our recipes prioritize fresh, whole ingredients to help you stay healthy and energized.
- **Time-Saving Tips:** Learn how to batch cook, layer for freshness, and store your jars to keep your meals fresh all week long.
- **Eco-Friendly Solutions:** Using reusable glass jars reduces waste and helps the environment.
- **Inspiration and Creativity:** Discover new flavor combinations and creative ways to enjoy your meals.

We're thrilled to have you join us on this culinary journey. Let's get started with some amazing meals in a jar that will make your life easier and more delicious. Happy cooking!

Benefits of Jar Meals

Embracing the concept of jar meals can transform your approach to eating and meal preparation. Here are some compelling reasons why you should consider incorporating jar meals into your daily routine:

1. Portability

Jar meals are incredibly portable, making them ideal for busy lifestyles. Glass jars are sturdy and spill-proof, fitting easily into bags, backpacks, or lunch boxes. Whether you're heading to work, school, or a picnic, you can take your nutritious meals with you wherever you go.

2. Portion Control

One of the biggest challenges in maintaining a healthy diet is managing portion sizes. Jars help you control your portions effortlessly. By using jars of a standard size, you can ensure you're eating the right amount without overindulging. This is particularly useful for those who are watching their calorie intake or following specific dietary plans.

3. Freshness

Airtight glass jars keep your meals fresh and crisp for longer periods. When properly sealed, these jars prevent air and moisture from spoiling your food. This means you can prepare your meals in advance without worrying about them losing their taste or texture. Fresh ingredients stay vibrant and delicious, giving you a restaurant-quality meal every time.

4. Eco-Friendly

Using reusable glass jars is an excellent way to reduce your environmental footprint. Unlike disposable plastic containers, glass jars can be used over and over again, minimizing waste. They are also free from harmful chemicals found in some plastics, making them a healthier choice for storing your food.

5. Visual Appeal

Meals in jars are not only practical but also visually appealing. The layered presentation of ingredients makes each meal look appetizing and colorful. This aesthetic appeal can make your meals more enjoyable and can even encourage picky eaters to try new foods. Plus, they're perfect for sharing on social media to inspire others with your culinary creations.

6. Time-Saving

Jar meals are a game-changer for time management. By prepping your meals in advance, you can save significant time during the week. Spend a couple of hours on the weekend preparing your jars, and you'll have ready-to-eat meals for days. This is especially beneficial for those with hectic schedules who want to avoid the daily hassle of cooking.

7. Versatility

The versatility of jar meals is one of their greatest strengths. You can create a wide range of dishes, from breakfasts and lunches to dinners and snacks. Whether you prefer savory salads, hearty grain bowls, or sweet desserts, there's a jar meal for every taste and dietary preference. The possibilities are endless, allowing you to keep your meals interesting and varied.

8. Budget-Friendly

Preparing meals in jars can be cost-effective. Buying ingredients in bulk and preparing your meals at home is often cheaper than eating out or buying pre-packaged foods. Additionally, jar meals help you make the most of leftovers, reducing food waste and stretching your grocery budget further.

9. Healthier Eating Habits

When you prepare meals in jars, you have complete control over the ingredients. This allows you to make healthier choices by incorporating fresh, whole foods and avoiding processed ingredients. You can tailor your meals to meet your nutritional needs and preferences, ensuring balanced and healthy diet.

10. Stress Reduction

Knowing that you have delicious, healthy meals ready to go can significantly reduce the stress of meal planning and preparation. It simplifies your daily routine, giving you more time to focu on other important aspects of your life. Plus, having a jar meal waiting for you can be a comforting thought on a busy day.

With all these benefits, it's easy to see why jar meals are becoming a popular choice for so man people. They offer a convenient, healthy, and enjoyable way to manage your meals, making it easier to stick to your dietary goals and enjoy the process of eating well.

How to Use This Book

Welcome to your guide to creating delicious and nutritious meals in jars. This book is structure to make your cooking experience as simple and enjoyable as possible. Here's how to navigate and make the most out of it:

1. Understanding the Structure

The book is organized into chapters based on meal types and themes. Each chapter is filled wit recipes tailored to specific times of the day or dietary needs. Here's a quick overview of what you'll find:

- **Breakfast Jars**: Start your day with energizing and filling options.
- **Lunch Jars**: Fresh and hearty meals perfect for midday.
- **Dinner Jars**: Satisfying and flavorful dishes to end your day.
- **Snack Jars**: Quick bites to keep you going.
- **Dessert Jars**: Sweet treats to indulge in.
- **Kid-Friendly Jars**: Fun and nutritious meals for the little ones.
- **Fitness and Wellness Jars**: High-protein and detox options.
- **Seasonal Jars**: Recipes based on seasonal ingredients.
- **Special Occasion Jars**: Meals for holidays and celebrations.
- **Dietary-Specific Jars**: Gluten-free, dairy-free, vegan, and more.
- **Meal Prep and Storage Tips**: Techniques to keep your meals fresh.
- **Ingredient Substitutions and Customizations**: Ideas to make each recipe your own.
- **Advanced Techniques and Tips**: For those who want to take their jar meals to the next level.
- **Budget-Friendly Jars**: Cost-effective recipes to save money.
- **Inspirational Stories and Testimonials**: Real-life success stories and tips from the community.

2. Recipe Layout

Each recipe is designed to be easy to follow, with clear instructions and readily available ingredients. Here's how each recipe is laid out:

- **Title**: The name of the recipe.
- **Introduction**: A brief description of the dish.
- **Ingredients**: A list of what you'll need, including specific quantities.
- **Instructions**: Step-by-step directions to guide you through the preparation.
- **Tips and Variations**: Additional suggestions to customize the recipe or enhance its flavor.

3. Icons and Symbols

To make navigation easier, the book uses icons and symbols to highlight key aspects of each recipe, such as:

- **Time Required**: Indicates the total time needed to prepare the dish.
- **Dietary Tags**: Labels like gluten-free, vegan, low-carb, etc.
- **Skill Level**: Indicates whether the recipe is beginner, intermediate, or advanced.

4. Meal Prep and Storage Tips

The "Meal Prep and Storage Tips" chapter provides essential advice on how to prepare and store your jar meals effectively. Learn about batch cooking, proper layering techniques to keep ingredients fresh, and best practices for storing and transporting your jars.

5. Customizing Recipes

The "Ingredient Substitutions and Customizations" chapter is your go-to resource for adapting recipes to fit your personal tastes or dietary requirements. Whether you need to swap an ingredient due to an allergy or want to try a new flavor combination, this section has you covered.

6. Exploring Advanced Techniques

For those who are more adventurous or experienced in the kitchen, the "Advanced Techniques and Tips" chapter offers ways to elevate your jar meals. From fermenting and pickling to using sous-vide methods, this section provides new culinary skills to explore.

7. Budgeting and Economizing

If you're looking to save money, the "Budget-Friendly Jars" chapter offers recipes that are cost-effective without sacrificing taste or nutrition. Learn how to make the most of inexpensive ingredients and reduce food waste.

8.

Before you dive into the recipes, here are a few final tips:

- **Read Through the Recipe**: Before starting, read the entire recipe to understand the steps and prepare all the ingredients.
- **Prep Ahead**: Take advantage of meal prep techniques to save time during the week.
- **Experiment and Have Fun**: Don't be afraid to experiment with flavors and ingredients to make each meal uniquely yours.

With this guide in hand, you're ready to embark on a journey of easy, delicious, and healthy eating. Enjoy the process of making and savoring your meals in a jar!

Essential Tools and Ingredients

Before you start creating your delicious meals in jars, it's important to have the right tools and ingredients on hand. This section will guide you through the essentials you'll need to make the most out of this cookbook.

Essential Tools

1. Glass Jars

- **Mason Jars:** These are the most popular choice for jar meals. They come in various sizes (typically 8 oz, 16 oz, and 32 oz) and are perfect for layering ingredients.

- **Lids and Bands:** Ensure you have airtight lids to keep your meals fresh. Reusable plastic lids are also a great option for convenience.

2. Measuring Cups and Spoons

Accurate measurements are key to following recipes, especially when it comes to layering ingredients. Invest in a good set of measuring cups and spoons.

3. Sharp Knives and Cutting Board

A sharp knife and a sturdy cutting board make chopping fruits, vegetables, and other ingredients easier and safer.

4. Mixing Bowls

Various sizes of mixing bowls will help you combine ingredients before layering them in jars.

5. Blender or Food Processor

For smoothies, purees, and certain dressings, a blender or food processor is essential.

6. Cooking Pots and Pans

Some recipes may require cooking ingredients before assembling them in jars. Basic pots and pans will suffice.

7. Funnels

A wide-mouth funnel can make transferring ingredients into jars less messy and more efficient.

8. Spoons and Spatulas

Having a variety of spoons and spatulas helps in mixing and transferring ingredients smoothly.

Essential Ingredients

1. Grains and Pasta

- **Quinoa, Rice, and Couscous:** These grains form the base for many jar meals.
- **Pasta:** Choose whole grain or gluten-free options as per your dietary needs.

2. Proteins

- **Legumes:** Beans, lentils, and chickpeas are excellent plant-based protein sources.

- **Meat and Poultry:** Pre-cooked chicken, beef, and turkey are convenient for adding to jars.
- **Seafood:** Canned or pre-cooked fish like tuna and salmon.
- **Tofu and Tempeh:** Great for vegetarian and vegan options.

3. Fresh Vegetables

- **Leafy Greens:** Spinach, kale, and arugula are nutrient-dense and great for salads.
- **Root Vegetables:** Carrots, beets, and sweet potatoes add flavor and texture.
- **Cruciferous Vegetables:** Broccoli, cauliflower, and Brussels sprouts for added crunch.

4. Fresh Fruits

- **Berries:** Strawberries, blueberries, and raspberries are perfect for breakfast jars and desserts.
- **Citrus Fruits:** Oranges, lemons, and limes add zest and freshness.
- **Tropical Fruits:** Pineapples, mangoes, and kiwis for a sweet touch.

5. Dairy and Dairy Alternatives

- **Yogurt:** Greek yogurt or dairy-free alternatives for breakfast and snack jars.
- **Cheese:** Feta, mozzarella, and cheddar for savory meals.
- **Milk and Milk Alternatives:** Almond milk, coconut milk, and regular milk for smoothies and puddings.

6. Nuts and Seeds

- **Almonds, Walnuts, and Pecans:** For added crunch and nutrition.
- **Chia Seeds, Flaxseeds, and Hemp Seeds:** For boosting the nutritional content.

7. Oils and Vinegars

- **Olive Oil and Coconut Oil:** Healthy fats for cooking and dressings.
- **Balsamic Vinegar, Apple Cider Vinegar, and Red Wine Vinegar:** For flavorful dressings and marinades.

8. Herbs and Spices

- **Fresh Herbs:** Basil, cilantro, and parsley for fresh flavor.
- **Dried Spices:** Cumin, paprika, and turmeric to enhance the taste of your meals.
- **Salt and Pepper:** Basic seasonings for almost every recipe.

9. Sweeteners

- **Honey and Maple Syrup:** Natural sweeteners for breakfast jars and desserts.
- **Agave Nectar and Stevia:** Alternative sweeteners for those reducing sugar intake.

10. Miscellaneous

- **Broth and Stock:** Vegetable, chicken, or beef broth for soups and savory dishes.
- **Canned Goods:** Tomatoes, beans, and corn for quick and easy additions.

Final Tips

- **Quality Over Quantity:** Invest in high-quality ingredients and tools. They make a noticeable difference in the taste and ease of preparation.
- **Stay Organized:** Keep your pantry and kitchen organized. Knowing where everything is will save you time and effort.
- **Prep Ahead:** Wash and chop vegetables, cook grains, and prepare proteins in advance to streamline the jar assembly process.

With these essential tools and ingredients, you are well-equipped to dive into the world of meals in a jar. Let's start creating some amazing recipes!

Chapter 1: Breakfast Jars 1.1.

Classic Overnight Oats 1.2.

Introduction

Overnight oats are a staple breakfast jar that is both simple to make and incredibly versatile. This classic version serves as a base, allowing you to customize it with your favorite fruits, nuts, and flavorings. Perfect for busy mornings, these oats are prepared the night before, so you can grab and go with ease.

Ingredients

- 1/2 cup old-fashioned rolled oats
- 1/2 cup milk (dairy or non-dairy)
- 1/4 cup Greek yogurt (or dairy-free yogurt)
- 1 tablespoon chia seeds
- 1-2 teaspoons honey or maple syrup (optional, for sweetness)
- 1/4 teaspoon vanilla extract
- Pinch of salt
- Toppings of your choice: fresh fruits, nuts, seeds, nut butter, etc.

Instructions

1. **Prepare the Base:**

- In a clean mason jar (16 oz recommended), combine the rolled oats, milk, Greek yogurt, chia seeds, honey or maple syrup (if using), vanilla extract, and a pinch of salt.

2. **Mix Ingredients:**

- Stir well to ensure all ingredients are thoroughly combined. The chia seeds might clump together, so make sure to break them up as you mix.

3. **Seal and Refrigerate:**

- Secure the lid on the jar and place it in the refrigerator. Let it sit overnight or for at least 4-6 hours. This allows the oats and chia seeds to absorb the liquid and soften.

4. **Add Toppings:**

- In the morning, open the jar and give the oats a good stir. Add your favorite toppings such as fresh berries, sliced bananas, chopped nuts, seeds, or a dollop of nut butter.

5. **Enjoy:**

- Your classic overnight oats are ready to eat! You can enjoy them cold straight from the jar or heat them up in the microwave if you prefer a warm breakfast.

Tips and Variations

- **Flavor Boosters:** Add a spoonful of cocoa powder or a sprinkle of cinnamon for an extra flavor kick.
- **Protein Punch:** Stir in a scoop of protein powder or a tablespoon of nut butter for added protein.
- **Vegan Option:** Use a plant-based yogurt and milk to keep it vegan-friendly.
- **Texture Preferences:** Adjust the amount of liquid based on how thick or thin you like your oats. More liquid will result in a thinner consistency, while less liquid will make it thicker.

Nutrition Information (Approximate per serving)

- **Calories:** 250
- **Protein:** 10g
- **Carbohydrates:** 40g
- **Fat:** 8g
- **Fiber:** 6g
- **Sugar:** 8g

Conclusion

Classic overnight oats are a fantastic way to start your day with a nutritious and satisfying meal. Easy to prepare and endlessly customizable, they fit perfectly into any busy lifestyle. Experiment with different toppings and flavors to keep your breakfasts exciting and delicious.

Berry Yogurt Parfait 1.3

Introduction

The **Berry Yogurt Parfait** is a versatile and nutritious recipe that's perfect for breakfast or a healthy snack. This chapter will walk you through creating a fresh and delicious parfait, layered with creamy yogurt, fresh berries, and crunchy granola. Not only does this parfait satisfy your taste buds, but it also provides a nutritious boost to your day.

Ingredients

For the basic parfait:

- 1 cup Greek yogurt (can be substituted with natural or vegan yogurt)
- 1/2 cup fresh berries (such as strawberries, blueberries, raspberries)
- 1/4 cup granola

For added flavor:

- 1 tablespoon honey or maple syrup
- 1/2 teaspoon vanilla extract
- 1/4 cup chia seeds (optional, for added thickness)

For garnish:

- Fresh mint leaves
- Extra berries
- A pinch of cinnamon or ginger powder

Preparation

1. **Prepare the Ingredients:**

   - Wash and dry the fresh berries thoroughly. If using frozen berries, thaw them at room temperature and drain any excess water.
2. **Prepare the Yogurt:**

   - In a bowl, mix the Greek yogurt with honey (or maple syrup) and vanilla extract. If you're using chia seeds, stir them into the yogurt mixture for added thickness and texture.
3. **Layer the Parfait:**

   - In a jar or glass, start by adding a layer of yogurt.
   - Next, add a layer of fresh berries.
   - Follow with a layer of granola.
   - Repeat the layers until you reach the top of the jar or glass.
4. **Garnish and Serve:**

- Top the parfait with a few extra berries and a sprig of fresh mint.
- Sprinkle a pinch of cinnamon or ginger powder if desired.
- Serve immediately or cover and refrigerate for up to 2 days.

Tips and Variations

- **For a Creamier Texture:** Use full-fat Greek yogurt or a plant-based alternative with added creaminess.
- **For Extra Crunch:** Add nuts or seeds in between the granola layers.
- **For Seasonal Variations:** Swap out the berries for seasonal fruits like peaches, apples, or pears depending on availability.

Nutritional Information

Each serving of this Berry Yogurt Parfait provides a good balance of protein, fiber, and antioxidants. Greek yogurt offers a protein boost, while the berries provide vitamins and antioxidants. Granola adds a satisfying crunch and fiber, making this parfait a wholesome and well-rounded meal.

Conclusion

The Berry Yogurt Parfait is not just a treat for the taste buds; it's a convenient and healthful option that can be customized to your liking. Experiment with different fruits, add-ins, and flavorings to make it your own. Whether enjoyed as a hearty breakfast or a midday snack, this parfait will keep you satisfied and energized.

Chia Seed Pudding Varieties 1.4.

Introduction

Chia seed pudding is a delightful, versatile, and nutritious option that's easy to prepare and customize. This chapter explores various chia seed pudding recipes, each offering a unique twist on the basic chia pudding formula. Packed with fiber, protein, and omega-3 fatty acids, chia seed pudding is not only good for you but also incredibly adaptable to different flavors and dietary preferences.

Basic Chia Seed Pudding Recipe

Ingredients:

- 1/4 cup chia seeds
- 1 cup milk (dairy or plant-based)
- 1-2 tablespoons sweetener (honey, maple syrup, agave nectar, or your choice)

- 1/2 teaspoon vanilla extract (optional)

Instructions:

1. **Combine Ingredients:** In a jar or bowl, mix the chia seeds, milk, sweetener, and vanilla extract until well combined.
2. **Refrigerate:** Cover and refrigerate for at least 4 hours or overnight, allowing the chia seeds to absorb the liquid and form a gel-like consistency.
3. **Stir and Serve:** Stir the pudding before serving. Add your favorite toppings or mix-ins.

Chia Seed Pudding Varieties

1. Berry Bliss Pudding

Ingredients:

- 1/4 cup chia seeds
- 1 cup almond milk (or milk of your choice)
- 1 tablespoon maple syrup
- 1/2 teaspoon vanilla extract
- 1/2 cup mixed berries (strawberries, blueberries, raspberries)

Instructions:

1. **Prepare Pudding Base:** Follow the basic chia seed pudding recipe.
2. **Add Fruit:** Once the pudding has set, layer it with fresh berries.
3. **Serve:** Top with additional berries and a dollop of yogurt if desired.

2. Chocolate Chia Pudding

Ingredients:

- 1/4 cup chia seeds
- 1 cup coconut milk
- 2 tablespoons cocoa powder
- 2 tablespoons honey or maple syrup
- 1/2 teaspoon vanilla extract

Instructions:

1. **Mix Ingredients:** Combine chia seeds, coconut milk, cocoa powder, honey, and vanilla extract.
2. **Chill:** Refrigerate for at least 4 hours or overnight.
3. **Serve:** Garnish with chocolate shavings or fresh fruit.

3. Tropical Coconut Chia Pudding

Ingredients:

- 1/4 cup chia seeds
- 1 cup coconut milk

- 1 tablespoon honey
- 1/2 teaspoon vanilla extract
- 1/2 cup diced mango
- 1/4 cup shredded coconut

Instructions:

1. **Prepare Pudding Base:** Mix chia seeds with coconut milk, honey, and vanilla extract.
2. **Layer with Fruit:** After setting, layer with diced mango and sprinkle shredded coconut on top.
3. **Serve:** Add a few mint leaves for extra freshness.

4. Matcha Green Tea Pudding

Ingredients:

- 1/4 cup chia seeds
- 1 cup almond milk
- 1 tablespoon honey or agave syrup
- 1 teaspoon matcha green tea powder
- 1/2 teaspoon vanilla extract

Instructions:

1. **Combine Ingredients:** Whisk chia seeds, almond milk, honey, matcha powder, and vanilla extract together.
2. **Refrigerate:** Let it set for at least 4 hours or overnight.
3. **Serve:** Top with a sprinkle of extra matcha powder and a few berries if desired.

5. Apple Cinnamon Chia Pudding

Ingredients:

- 1/4 cup chia seeds
- 1 cup oat milk
- 1 tablespoon maple syrup
- 1/2 teaspoon vanilla extract
- 1/2 teaspoon ground cinnamon
- 1/2 cup diced apples

Instructions:

1. **Prepare Pudding Base:** Mix chia seeds with oat milk, maple syrup, vanilla extract, and cinnamon.
2. **Add Apples:** After setting, stir in diced apples.
3. **Serve:** Top with a sprinkle of extra cinnamon and a handful of granola if desired.

Tips for Perfect Chia Seed Pudding

- **Consistency:** For a thicker pudding, use more chia seeds. For a thinner texture, increase the amount of liquid.

- **Flavor Variations:** Experiment with different spices, extracts, or flavorings to customize your pudding.
- **Toppings:** Fresh fruit, nuts, seeds, or a drizzle of nut butter can add texture and flavor to your chia pudding.

Nutritional Benefits

Chia seeds are rich in omega-3 fatty acids, fiber, and protein, making chia seed pudding a nutritious choice. The various pudding varieties incorporate fruits, cocoa, or matcha to add additional vitamins, antioxidants, and flavor.

Conclusion

Chia seed pudding is a wonderfully flexible dish that can be tailored to suit your taste and dietary needs. Whether you prefer a fruity, chocolatey, or exotic twist, these recipes provide a delicious and healthful way to enjoy this superfood. Feel free to experiment and make these puddings your own!

Smoothie Jars 1.5.

Introduction

Smoothie jars offer a convenient and delicious way to enjoy a nutritious smoothie on the go. By preparing your smoothies in advance and storing them in jars, you save time and ensure you have a healthy option ready whenever you need it. This chapter explores how to create and store smoothie jars that maintain their freshness and flavor, along with a variety of scrumptious recipes to get you started.

Basic Smoothie Jar Preparation

Ingredients:

- Fresh or frozen fruits (such as berries, bananas, mangoes)
- Leafy greens (like spinach or kale, if desired)
- Liquid (milk, almond milk, coconut water, or juice)
- Add-ins (like yogurt, protein powder, or flax seeds)

Instructions:

1. **Layer Ingredients:** Start by adding the ingredients that are least likely to spoil, such as fruits, vegetables, and protein powders, at the bottom of the jar.
2. **Add Liquids:** Pour your chosen liquid on top of the dry ingredients. This helps to keep the ingredients fresh and prevents separation.
3. **Seal and Store:** Close the jar tightly and refrigerate. Smoothie jars can typically be stored in the refrigerator for up to 3 days.

Smoothie Jar Recipes

1. Berry Green Smoothie

Ingredients:

- 1/2 cup fresh spinach
- 1/2 cup mixed berries (blueberries, raspberries, strawberries)
- 1/2 banana
- 1 cup almond milk
- 1 tablespoon chia seeds

Instructions:

1. **Layer Ingredients:** Add spinach, berries, and banana to the jar.
2. **Add Liquid and Seeds:** Pour almond milk over the fruit and add chia seeds.
3. **Store:** Refrigerate for up to 3 days. Shake well before serving or blend as desired.

2. Tropical Sunrise Smoothie

Ingredients:

- 1/2 cup diced mango
- 1/2 cup pineapple chunks
- 1/2 banana
- 1/2 cup coconut water
- 1/2 cup Greek yogurt

Instructions:

1. **Layer Ingredients:** Place mango, pineapple, and banana in the jar.
2. **Add Liquid and Yogurt:** Pour coconut water and add Greek yogurt.
3. **Store:** Keep in the refrigerator for up to 3 days. Shake or blend before enjoying.

3. Chocolate Peanut Butter Smoothie

Ingredients:

- 1/2 cup banana
- 2 tablespoons natural peanut butter
- 1 tablespoon cocoa powder
- 1 cup milk (dairy or plant-based)
- 1 tablespoon flax seeds

Instructions:

1. **Layer Ingredients:** Add banana, peanut butter, and cocoa powder to the jar.
2. **Add Liquid and Seeds:** Pour milk over the top and add flax seeds.
3. **Store:** Refrigerate for up to 3 days. Shake or blend before serving.

4. Apple Cinnamon Smoothie

Ingredients:

- 1/2 apple, diced
- 1/2 banana
- 1/2 cup spinach
- 1 cup oat milk
- 1/2 teaspoon ground cinnamon

Instructions:

1. **Layer Ingredients:** Add apple, banana, and spinach to the jar.
2. **Add Liquid and Cinnamon:** Pour oat milk over the top and sprinkle with cinnamon.
3. **Store:** Keep in the refrigerator for up to 3 days. Shake or blend before consuming.

5. Avocado Mint Smoothie

Ingredients:

- 1/2 avocado
- 1/2 cup pineapple chunks
- 1/4 cup fresh mint leaves
- 1 cup coconut milk
- 1 tablespoon honey

Instructions:

1. **Layer Ingredients:** Add avocado, pineapple, and mint leaves to the jar.
2. **Add Liquid and Sweetener:** Pour coconut milk over the top and add honey.
3. **Store:** Refrigerate for up to 3 days. Shake or blend before serving.

Tips for Perfect Smoothie Jars

- **Layering:** Always layer the ingredients from the most liquid to the driest to prevent spoilage and maintain freshness.
- **Freezing:** For longer storage, freeze smoothie jars. Just remember to leave some space at the top for expansion.
- **Thawing:** When ready to use, thaw frozen smoothie jars in the refrigerator overnight or blend directly from frozen for a thicker consistency.
- **Shake Well:** If you prefer a thicker texture, blend the smoothie jar contents. If you like a lighter texture, shaking the jar will suffice.

Nutritional Benefits

Smoothie jars are a fantastic way to incorporate a variety of fruits, vegetables, and other nutritious ingredients into your diet. By preparing them in advance, you ensure that you have a quick, healthful meal or snack ready whenever you need it.

Conclusion

Smoothie jars are a practical and enjoyable solution for busy lifestyles, providing a healthy, customizable option that's both convenient and delicious. Experiment with different combinations to find your favorite flavors, and make the most out of your smoothie preparation by keeping these jars stocked and ready to go.

Nut Butter and Fruit Jars 1.6.

Introduction

Nut butter and fruit jars are a convenient and nutritious way to enjoy a satisfying snack or light meal. Combining creamy nut butters with fresh or dried fruits creates a perfect balance of protein, healthy fats, and natural sugars. This chapter explores how to prepare and store nut butter and fruit jars, along with a variety of delicious combinations to keep your taste buds happy and your body fueled.

Basic Nut Butter and Fruit Jar Preparation

Ingredients:

- Nut butters (such as almond butter, peanut butter, cashew butter, or sunflower seed butter)
- Fresh or dried fruits (like apples, pears, bananas, berries, or raisins)
- Optional add-ins (such as seeds, granola, or honey)

Instructions:

1. **Layer Ingredients:** Start by adding nut butter to the bottom of the jar. This helps to prevent the fruits from becoming mushy and keeps the nut butter from separating.
2. **Add Fruits:** Layer your chosen fruits on top of the nut butter.
3. **Add Optional Ingredients:** If desired, add seeds, granola, or a drizzle of honey.
4. **Seal and Store:** Close the jar tightly and refrigerate. These jars can typically be stored for up to 3 days.

Nut Butter and Fruit Jar Recipes

1. Apple Almond Butter Delight

Ingredients:

- 2 tablespoons almond butter
- 1 medium apple, sliced
- 1 tablespoon chia seeds
- 1 teaspoon honey (optional)

Instructions:

1. **Layer Almond Butter:** Spoon almond butter into the bottom of the jar.
2. **Add Apple Slices:** Arrange apple slices on top of the nut butter.
3. **Sprinkle Chia Seeds:** Add chia seeds and drizzle with honey if desired.
4. **Store:** Refrigerate for up to 3 days.

2. Banana Peanut Butter Bliss

Ingredients:

- 2 tablespoons peanut butter
- 1 banana, sliced
- 1 tablespoon granola
- 1/4 teaspoon cinnamon

Instructions:

1. **Layer Peanut Butter:** Add peanut butter to the bottom of the jar.
2. **Add Banana Slices:** Layer banana slices on top of the peanut butter.
3. **Top with Granola and Cinnamon:** Sprinkle granola and a dash of cinnamon on top.
4. **Store:** Refrigerate for up to 3 days.

3. Pear Cashew Butter Crunch

Ingredients:

- 2 tablespoons cashew butter
- 1 medium pear, sliced
- 1 tablespoon pumpkin seeds
- 1 tablespoon dried cranberries

Instructions:

1. **Layer Cashew Butter:** Place cashew butter at the bottom of the jar.
2. **Add Pear Slices:** Arrange pear slices on top.
3. **Add Seeds and Cranberries:** Top with pumpkin seeds and dried cranberries.
4. **Store:** Refrigerate for up to 3 days.

4. Berry Sunflower Seed Butter

Ingredients:

- 2 tablespoons sunflower seed butter
- 1/2 cup mixed berries (blueberries, strawberries, raspberries)
- 1 tablespoon flax seeds
- 1 tablespoon shredded coconut

Instructions:

1. **Layer Sunflower Seed Butter:** Spoon sunflower seed butter into the jar.
2. **Add Berries:** Layer mixed berries on top.
3. **Sprinkle Seeds and Coconut:** Add flax seeds and shredded coconut.

4. **Store:** Refrigerate for up to 3 days.

5. Peach Almond Butter Fusion

Ingredients:

- 2 tablespoons almond butter
- 1 medium peach, sliced
- 1 tablespoon sliced almonds
- 1 tablespoon honey (optional)

Instructions:

1. **Layer Almond Butter:** Start with almond butter at the bottom of the jar.
2. **Add Peach Slices:** Layer peach slices on top.
3. **Top with Almonds and Honey:** Sprinkle sliced almonds and drizzle with honey if desired.
4. **Store:** Refrigerate for up to 3 days.

Tips for Perfect Nut Butter and Fruit Jars

- **Texture:** Use fresh fruits for a crisp texture or dried fruits for a chewy consistency. Adjust based on your preference.
- **Nut Butter Choice:** Experiment with different nut butters to find your favorite combination. Each nut butter has its own unique flavor and texture.
- **Layering:** Adding nut butter to the bottom helps to prevent fruits from becoming soggy and ensures a more enjoyable texture.
- **Storage:** Keep jars tightly sealed and refrigerated. For longer storage, consider freezing jars, but be mindful that the texture may change slightly upon thawing.

Nutritional Benefits

Nut butters are rich in healthy fats and proteins, while fruits provide essential vitamins, minerals, and natural sugars. This combination offers a balanced snack that supports energy levels and keeps you satisfied.

Conclusion

Nut butter and fruit jars are a versatile and delicious option for those looking for a quick, nutritious meal or snack. With countless combinations to suit any taste preference, these jars offer an easy way to enjoy a wholesome, satisfying treat. Experiment with different fruits and nut butters to create your perfect jar, and enjoy the convenience of having a healthy option read at all times.

Savory Breakfast Jars

Introduction

Savory breakfast jars offer a delicious and convenient alternative to traditional sweet breakfasts. Packed with proteins, vegetables, and grains, these jars are perfect for starting your day on a hearty and satisfying note. This chapter will guide you through creating a variety of savory breakfast jars that are both nutritious and easy to prepare, ensuring you have a flavorful and balanced meal ready whenever you need it.

Basic Savory Breakfast Jar Preparation

Ingredients:

- Base ingredients (such as cooked grains, beans, or potatoes)
- Protein sources (like eggs, tofu, or lean meats)
- Vegetables (fresh or cooked, such as spinach, bell peppers, or tomatoes)
- Flavorings and seasonings (herbs, spices, cheese, or sauces)
- Optional toppings (avocado, nuts, or seeds)

Instructions:

1. **Prepare the Base:** Start with a base ingredient such as cooked quinoa, brown rice, or roasted potatoes. This forms the foundation of your jar.
2. **Add Protein:** Layer in your chosen protein source. Options include hard-boiled eggs, cooked chicken, or sautéed tofu.
3. **Include Vegetables:** Add a variety of vegetables, either raw or cooked. Fresh spinach, cherry tomatoes, or sautéed bell peppers work well.
4. **Season and Flavor:** Season with herbs, spices, or cheese. You can also add a small amount of sauce or dressing for extra flavor.
5. **Top and Store:** Finish with optional toppings if desired, seal the jar tightly, and refrigerate. Savory breakfast jars can typically be stored for up to 3 days.

Savory Breakfast Jar Recipes

1. Southwest Quinoa Jar

Ingredients:

- 1/2 cup cooked quinoa
- 1/4 cup black beans
- 1/4 cup corn kernels
- 1/4 cup diced tomatoes
- 1/4 cup shredded cheddar cheese
- 1 tablespoon chopped cilantro
- 1/4 teaspoon cumin

Instructions:

1. **Layer Quinoa:** Start with cooked quinoa at the bottom of the jar.
2. **Add Beans and Corn:** Layer black beans and corn on top.
3. **Add Tomatoes and Cheese:** Add diced tomatoes and shredded cheddar cheese.
4. **Season:** Sprinkle with chopped cilantro and cumin.
5. **Store:** Refrigerate for up to 3 days. Reheat or enjoy cold.

2. Mediterranean Breakfast Jar

Ingredients:

- 1/2 cup cooked farro or brown rice
- 1/4 cup diced cucumbers
- 1/4 cup cherry tomatoes, halved
- 1/4 cup kalamata olives, sliced
- 1/4 cup crumbled feta cheese
- 1 tablespoon chopped fresh basil
- 1 tablespoon olive oil

Instructions:

1. **Layer Farro:** Start with farro or brown rice at the bottom of the jar.
2. **Add Vegetables and Olives:** Layer cucumbers, cherry tomatoes, and kalamata olives.
3. **Add Feta Cheese:** Sprinkle crumbled feta cheese on top.
4. **Season:** Drizzle with olive oil and top with fresh basil.
5. **Store:** Refrigerate for up to 3 days. Reheat if desired or enjoy cold.

3. Hearty Breakfast Potatoes

Ingredients:

- 1/2 cup roasted diced potatoes
- 1/4 cup cooked sausage or bacon, chopped
- 1/4 cup sautéed bell peppers
- 1/4 cup shredded mozzarella cheese
- 1 tablespoon chopped chives
- 1/4 teaspoon paprika

Instructions:

1. **Layer Potatoes:** Start with roasted diced potatoes in the jar.
2. **Add Sausage or Bacon:** Layer cooked sausage or bacon on top.
3. **Add Peppers and Cheese:** Add sautéed bell peppers and shredded mozzarella cheese.
4. **Season:** Sprinkle with chopped chives and paprika.
5. **Store:** Refrigerate for up to 3 days. Reheat before eating.

4. Spinach and Feta Egg Jar

Ingredients:

- 2 large hard-boiled eggs, sliced
- 1/2 cup fresh spinach leaves
- 1/4 cup crumbled feta cheese

- 1/4 cup diced red bell peppers
- 1 tablespoon chopped fresh dill
- Salt and pepper to taste

Instructions:

1. **Layer Spinach:** Place fresh spinach leaves at the bottom of the jar.
2. **Add Eggs and Veggies:** Layer sliced hard-boiled eggs, crumbled feta cheese, and diced red bell peppers.
3. **Season:** Add chopped dill and season with salt and pepper.
4. **Store:** Refrigerate for up to 3 days. Enjoy cold or at room temperature.

5. Breakfast Burrito Jar

Ingredients:

- 1/2 cup cooked brown rice
- 1/4 cup black beans
- 1/4 cup diced avocado
- 1/4 cup salsa
- 1/4 cup shredded cheese
- 1 tablespoon chopped green onions
- 1/4 teaspoon chili powder

Instructions:

1. **Layer Rice:** Start with cooked brown rice at the bottom of the jar.
2. **Add Beans and Avocado:** Layer black beans and diced avocado.
3. **Add Salsa and Cheese:** Pour salsa over the top and sprinkle with shredded cheese.
4. **Season:** Top with chopped green onions and chili powder.
5. **Store:** Refrigerate for up to 3 days. Reheat or enjoy cold.

Tips for Perfect Savory Breakfast Jars

- **Preparation:** Cook grains, proteins, and vegetables in advance to make assembly quicker and easier.
- **Layering:** Always place heavier items like grains or proteins at the bottom to prevent them from becoming soggy.
- **Seasoning:** Adjust seasonings according to your taste preferences and dietary needs.
- **Storage:** Ensure jars are tightly sealed to maintain freshness and prevent leaks.

Nutritional Benefits

Savory breakfast jars are a balanced and nutritious option that provides a mix of proteins, healthy fats, and carbohydrates. They are perfect for those who prefer a savory start to their day and offer a satisfying way to incorporate a variety of wholesome ingredients.

Conclusion

Savory breakfast jars are an excellent way to enjoy a hearty, nutritious meal on the go. With a variety of recipes to suit different tastes and dietary needs, these jars provide a convenient solution for busy mornings. Prepare them ahead of time and enjoy a satisfying breakfast that's both delicious and nourishing.

Chapter 2:

Lunch Jars 2.1.

Introduction

Lunch jars offer a practical and stylish solution for taking your meals on the go. These jars are perfect for busy workdays, school lunches, or a quick, nutritious meal at home. By layering ingredients thoughtfully, you can create balanced, flavorful, and easy-to-prepare lunches that stay fresh and appetizing. This chapter will guide you through the essentials of assembling lunc jars, and provide a variety of delicious recipes to inspire your midday meals.

Basic Lunch Jar Preparation

Ingredients:

- Base ingredients (such as grains, pasta, or legumes)
- Protein sources (like chicken, tofu, or beans)
- Vegetables (raw or cooked, such as bell peppers, cucumbers, or roasted carrots)
- Dressings and sauces (for added flavor and moisture)
- Optional add-ins (like cheese, nuts, or seeds)

Instructions:

1. **Layer Ingredients:** Begin by adding the ingredients that should remain at the bottom, such as sauces or dressings. This keeps the rest of the ingredients from becoming soggy
2. **Add Protein and Base:** Layer in your chosen protein and base ingredient (grains, pasta or legumes).
3. **Include Vegetables:** Add a variety of vegetables for texture and nutrition.
4. **Top and Store:** Finish with optional add-ins or garnishes, seal the jar tightly, and refrigerate. Lunch jars are typically good for up to 4 days.

Lunch Jar Recipes

1. Mediterranean Quinoa Jar

Ingredients:

- 1/4 cup hummus (bottom layer)
- 1/2 cup cooked quinoa
- 1/4 cup diced cucumbers
- 1/4 cup cherry tomatoes, halved
- 1/4 cup kalamata olives, sliced
- 1/4 cup crumbled feta cheese
- 1 tablespoon chopped fresh parsley

Instructions:

1. **Layer Hummus:** Start with a layer of hummus at the bottom of the jar.
2. **Add Quinoa:** Spoon cooked quinoa over the hummus.
3. **Add Vegetables:** Layer cucumbers, cherry tomatoes, and olives.
4. **Top with Cheese and Herbs:** Sprinkle with crumbled feta and fresh parsley.
5. **Store:** Refrigerate for up to 4 days. Shake before eating or serve with a spoon.

2. Asian Noodle Salad Jar

Ingredients:

- 2 tablespoons sesame dressing (bottom layer)
- 1/2 cup cooked soba noodles
- 1/4 cup shredded carrots
- 1/4 cup sliced bell peppers
- 1/4 cup edamame (shelled)
- 2 tablespoons chopped green onions
- 1 tablespoon sesame seeds

Instructions:

1. **Layer Dressing:** Begin with sesame dressing at the bottom.
2. **Add Noodles:** Layer cooked soba noodles on top of the dressing.
3. **Add Vegetables:** Add shredded carrots, bell peppers, and edamame.
4. **Top with Green Onions and Sesame Seeds:** Sprinkle with green onions and sesame seeds.
5. **Store:** Refrigerate for up to 4 days. Shake to mix before eating or serve cold.

3. Southwest Chicken Jar

Ingredients:

- 2 tablespoons salsa (bottom layer)
- 1/2 cup cooked brown rice
- 1/4 cup cooked chicken breast, shredded
- 1/4 cup black beans
- 1/4 cup corn kernels
- 1/4 cup diced avocado
- 1/4 cup shredded cheddar cheese
- 1 tablespoon chopped cilantro

Instructions:

1. **Layer Salsa:** Start with salsa at the bottom.
2. **Add Rice:** Layer cooked brown rice over the salsa.
3. **Add Chicken and Beans:** Layer shredded chicken and black beans.
4. **Add Corn and Avocado:** Add corn kernels and diced avocado.
5. **Top with Cheese and Cilantro:** Sprinkle with cheddar cheese and chopped cilantro.
6. **Store:** Refrigerate for up to 4 days. Reheat if desired or enjoy cold.

4. Greek Chicken Salad Jar

Ingredients:

- 2 tablespoons tzatziki sauce (bottom layer)
- 1/2 cup chopped cooked chicken breast
- 1/4 cup chopped cucumbers
- 1/4 cup cherry tomatoes, halved
- 1/4 cup red onion, thinly sliced
- 1/4 cup kalamata olives
- 1/4 cup crumbled feta cheese
- 1 tablespoon fresh dill

Instructions:

1. **Layer Tzatziki:** Start with tzatziki sauce at the bottom.
2. **Add Chicken:** Layer chopped chicken breast over the sauce.
3. **Add Vegetables:** Layer cucumbers, cherry tomatoes, red onion, and olives.
4. **Top with Cheese and Dill:** Sprinkle with crumbled feta and fresh dill.
5. **Store:** Refrigerate for up to 4 days. Shake before eating or enjoy cold.

5. Roasted Veggie and Hummus Jar

Ingredients:

- 1/4 cup hummus (bottom layer)
- 1/2 cup roasted vegetables (such as zucchini, bell peppers, and eggplant)
- 1/4 cup cooked farro or barley
- 1/4 cup chopped fresh spinach
- 1 tablespoon pine nuts
- 1 tablespoon grated Parmesan cheese

Instructions:

1. **Layer Hummus:** Start with hummus at the bottom of the jar.
2. **Add Roasted Vegetables:** Layer roasted vegetables on top.
3. **Add Farro or Barley:** Spoon cooked farro or barley over the vegetables.
4. **Add Spinach and Toppings:** Add chopped spinach, pine nuts, and grated Parmesan.
5. **Store:** Refrigerate for up to 4 days. Reheat if desired or serve cold.

Tips for Perfect Lunch Jars

- **Layering:** Start with sauces or dressings at the bottom to prevent sogginess. Layer heavier ingredients like grains or proteins next, followed by vegetables and lighter ingredients.
- **Portion Control:** Ensure you use the right jar size to accommodate your ingredients without overcrowding. A wide-mouth jar is often easier to pack and access.
- **Flavor Balance:** Use a mix of textures and flavors (crunchy, creamy, spicy, etc.) to make your lunch more enjoyable.
- **Storage:** Ensure jars are sealed tightly to keep ingredients fresh and prevent leaks.

Nutritional Benefits

Lunch jars are an excellent way to incorporate a balanced mix of proteins, vegetables, and grains into your diet. They provide a convenient way to ensure you're getting essential nutrients while managing portion sizes and avoiding unhealthy takeout options.

Conclusion

Lunch jars are a practical and enjoyable way to prepare and enjoy a balanced meal on the go. With a variety of recipes to choose from, you can easily customize your jars to suit your tastes and dietary needs. Prepare them in advance to ensure you have a healthy and delicious lunch ready whenever you need it.

Fresh Salads 2.2.

Fresh Salads 2.2

Introduction

Fresh salads are a versatile and nutritious option for a quick meal or a satisfying side dish. When prepared in jars, salads remain crisp and flavorful, making them perfect for meal prepping or taking on the go. This chapter will guide you through the essentials of creating fresh salad jars, offer a variety of recipes to suit different tastes, and provide tips for keeping your salads fresh and vibrant.

Basic Salad Jar Preparation

Ingredients:

- Base ingredients (such as lettuce, spinach, or mixed greens)
- Vegetables (like cucumbers, cherry tomatoes, or bell peppers)

- Protein sources (e.g., grilled chicken, chickpeas, or hard-boiled eggs)
- Add-ins (such as cheese, nuts, or seeds)
- Dressings (stored separately to keep the salad fresh)

Instructions:

1. **Layer Ingredients:** Start with the dressing at the bottom of the jar to keep the salad greens from becoming soggy.
2. **Add Harder Ingredients:** Layer vegetables and proteins that won't wilt, such as cucumbers, bell peppers, or beans.
3. **Add Greens:** Place the salad greens or leafy vegetables on top.
4. **Top and Store:** Finish with cheese, nuts, or seeds. Seal the jar tightly and refrigerate. Fresh salads in jars can typically be stored for up to 4 days.

Fresh Salad Jar Recipes

1. Classic Caesar Salad Jar

Ingredients:

- 2 tablespoons Caesar dressing (bottom layer)
- 1/2 cup cooked chicken breast, diced
- 1/4 cup cherry tomatoes, halved
- 1/4 cup croutons
- 1/4 cup shredded Parmesan cheese
- 1 cup romaine lettuce

Instructions:

1. **Layer Dressing:** Start with Caesar dressing at the bottom.
2. **Add Chicken:** Layer diced chicken breast over the dressing.
3. **Add Tomatoes:** Add cherry tomatoes on top of the chicken.
4. **Add Croutons and Cheese:** Add croutons and shredded Parmesan.
5. **Top with Lettuce:** Finish with romaine lettuce.
6. **Store:** Refrigerate for up to 4 days. Shake before eating or serve with a spoon.

2. Greek Salad Jar

Ingredients:

- 2 tablespoons Greek dressing (bottom layer)
- 1/4 cup diced cucumbers
- 1/4 cup cherry tomatoes, halved
- 1/4 cup kalamata olives
- 1/4 cup red onion, thinly sliced
- 1/4 cup crumbled feta cheese
- 1 cup mixed greens

Instructions:

1. **Layer Dressing:** Begin with Greek dressing at the bottom.

2. **Add Vegetables:** Layer cucumbers, cherry tomatoes, olives, and red onion.
3. **Add Cheese:** Sprinkle with crumbled feta cheese.
4. **Top with Greens:** Finish with mixed greens.
5. **Store:** Refrigerate for up to 4 days. Shake or toss before serving.

3. Southwest Quinoa Salad Jar

Ingredients:

- 2 tablespoons Southwest dressing (bottom layer)
- 1/2 cup cooked quinoa
- 1/4 cup black beans
- 1/4 cup corn kernels
- 1/4 cup diced red bell pepper
- 1/4 cup shredded cheddar cheese
- 1 cup chopped romaine lettuce

Instructions:

1. **Layer Dressing:** Start with Southwest dressing at the bottom.
2. **Add Quinoa and Beans:** Layer cooked quinoa and black beans.
3. **Add Corn and Peppers:** Add corn kernels and diced red bell pepper.
4. **Add Cheese:** Sprinkle with shredded cheddar cheese.
5. **Top with Lettuce:** Finish with chopped romaine lettuce.
6. **Store:** Refrigerate for up to 4 days. Shake before serving.

4. Mediterranean Chickpea Salad Jar

Ingredients:

- 2 tablespoons balsamic vinaigrette (bottom layer)
- 1/2 cup cooked chickpeas
- 1/4 cup diced cucumbers
- 1/4 cup cherry tomatoes, halved
- 1/4 cup kalamata olives
- 1/4 cup crumbled feta cheese
- 1 cup baby spinach

Instructions:

1. **Layer Dressing:** Begin with balsamic vinaigrette at the bottom.
2. **Add Chickpeas:** Layer cooked chickpeas over the dressing.
3. **Add Vegetables:** Add cucumbers, cherry tomatoes, and kalamata olives.
4. **Add Cheese:** Sprinkle with crumbled feta cheese.
5. **Top with Spinach:** Finish with baby spinach.
6. **Store:** Refrigerate for up to 4 days. Shake before serving.

5. Asian Noodle Salad Jar

Ingredients:

- 2 tablespoons sesame ginger dressing (bottom layer)

- 1/2 cup cooked soba noodles
- 1/4 cup shredded carrots
- 1/4 cup sliced bell peppers
- 1/4 cup edamame
- 2 tablespoons chopped green onions
- 1 tablespoon sesame seeds

Instructions:

1. **Layer Dressing:** Start with sesame ginger dressing at the bottom.
2. **Add Noodles:** Layer cooked soba noodles over the dressing.
3. **Add Vegetables:** Add shredded carrots, sliced bell peppers, and edamame.
4. **Add Toppings:** Sprinkle with chopped green onions and sesame seeds.
5. **Store:** Refrigerate for up to 4 days. Shake or toss before serving.

Tips for Perfect Fresh Salad Jars

- **Layering:** Always layer the dressing at the bottom to keep the greens crisp and fresh. Place heavier ingredients like proteins and grains next, followed by vegetables, and finish with leafy greens.
- **Freshness:** Use fresh, crisp vegetables and greens for the best texture and flavor. Avoid using ingredients that wilt quickly, like delicate herbs.
- **Dressing Separation:** To prevent sogginess, keep the dressing separate if you're not eating the salad immediately. You can use a small container or pour the dressing over the salad just before eating.
- **Portion Control:** Use the appropriate size jar to ensure that your salad ingredients are well distributed and not overcrowded.

Nutritional Benefits

Fresh salads are rich in vitamins, minerals, and antioxidants from the variety of vegetables and greens used. Adding proteins and healthy fats helps create a balanced meal that supports energy and satiety throughout the day.

Conclusion

Fresh salad jars are a fantastic way to enjoy a nutritious and flavorful meal with minimal preparation. With a range of recipes to suit different tastes and dietary preferences, these jars offer a convenient and healthful option for any meal. Prepare your salads in advance and enjoy the freshness and variety that these jarred creations provide.

Hearty Grain Bowls 2.3.

Introduction

Hearty grain bowls are a fantastic way to create a satisfying and nutritious meal in a jar. By combining wholesome grains with a variety of proteins, vegetables, and flavorful dressings, you can craft versatile and balanced meals that are both filling and delicious. This chapter will guide you through the essentials of assembling hearty grain bowls, provide a range of recipes, and offer tips for ensuring your bowls stay fresh and tasty.

Basic Hearty Grain Bowl Preparation

Ingredients:

- Grains (such as quinoa, brown rice, farro, or barley)
- Protein sources (like chicken, tofu, beans, or eggs)
- Vegetables (raw or cooked, including greens, roasted vegetables, or pickled items)
- Dressings or sauces (for added flavor)
- Optional toppings (cheese, nuts, seeds, or avocado)

Instructions:

1. **Prepare Grains:** Start with your chosen grain as the base of the bowl. Cook and let it cool before layering.
2. **Add Protein:** Layer in your protein source, whether it's cooked meat, tofu, or beans.
3. **Include Vegetables:** Add a variety of vegetables for color, texture, and nutrients.
4. **Dress and Top:** Drizzle with your preferred dressing or sauce and add optional toppings.
5. **Store:** Seal the jar tightly and refrigerate. Hearty grain bowls can typically be stored for up to 4 days.

Hearty Grain Bowl Recipes

1. Mediterranean Farro Bowl

Ingredients:

- 1/2 cup cooked farro
- 1/4 cup chickpeas, rinsed and drained
- 1/4 cup diced cucumbers
- 1/4 cup cherry tomatoes, halved
- 1/4 cup kalamata olives, sliced
- 1/4 cup crumbled feta cheese
- 2 tablespoons Greek dressing

Instructions:

1. **Layer Farro:** Start with cooked farro at the bottom of the jar.
2. **Add Chickpeas:** Layer chickpeas over the farro.
3. **Add Vegetables:** Add cucumbers, cherry tomatoes, and olives.

4. **Add Feta Cheese:** Sprinkle with crumbled feta cheese.
5. **Drizzle with Dressing:** Pour Greek dressing over the top.
6. **Store:** Refrigerate for up to 4 days. Shake before eating or serve with a spoon.

2. Asian-Inspired Rice Bowl

Ingredients:

- 1/2 cup cooked brown rice
- 1/4 cup edamame
- 1/4 cup shredded carrots
- 1/4 cup sliced bell peppers
- 1/4 cup cooked chicken or tofu, cubed
- 2 tablespoons sesame ginger dressing
- 1 tablespoon sesame seeds

Instructions:

1. **Layer Rice:** Start with cooked brown rice at the bottom of the jar.
2. **Add Vegetables and Protein:** Layer edamame, shredded carrots, bell peppers, and chicken or tofu.
3. **Drizzle with Dressing:** Pour sesame ginger dressing over the top.
4. **Top with Sesame Seeds:** Sprinkle with sesame seeds.
5. **Store:** Refrigerate for up to 4 days. Shake or toss before serving.

3. Southwest Quinoa Bowl

Ingredients:

- 1/2 cup cooked quinoa
- 1/4 cup black beans
- 1/4 cup corn kernels
- 1/4 cup diced red bell peppers
- 1/4 cup avocado, diced
- 1/4 cup shredded cheddar cheese
- 2 tablespoons Southwest dressing

Instructions:

1. **Layer Quinoa:** Start with cooked quinoa at the bottom of the jar.
2. **Add Beans and Corn:** Layer black beans and corn kernels.
3. **Add Vegetables:** Add diced red bell peppers and avocado.
4. **Add Cheese:** Sprinkle with shredded cheddar cheese.
5. **Drizzle with Dressing:** Pour Southwest dressing over the top.
6. **Store:** Refrigerate for up to 4 days. Shake before eating or enjoy cold.

4. Roasted Veggie Barley Bowl

Ingredients:

- 1/2 cup cooked barley
- 1/4 cup roasted sweet potatoes

- 1/4 cup roasted Brussels sprouts
- 1/4 cup chopped kale
- 1/4 cup crumbled goat cheese
- 2 tablespoons balsamic vinaigrette

Instructions:

1. **Layer Barley:** Start with cooked barley at the bottom of the jar.
2. **Add Roasted Vegetables:** Layer roasted sweet potatoes and Brussels sprouts.
3. **Add Kale:** Add chopped kale on top of the roasted vegetables.
4. **Add Cheese:** Sprinkle with crumbled goat cheese.
5. **Drizzle with Dressing:** Pour balsamic vinaigrette over the top.
6. **Store:** Refrigerate for up to 4 days. Shake before eating or serve with a spoon.

5. Greek Chicken and Rice Bowl

Ingredients:

- 1/2 cup cooked brown rice
- 1/4 cup grilled chicken breast, sliced
- 1/4 cup diced cucumbers
- 1/4 cup cherry tomatoes, halved
- 1/4 cup kalamata olives
- 1/4 cup crumbled feta cheese
- 2 tablespoons tzatziki sauce

Instructions:

1. **Layer Rice:** Start with cooked brown rice at the bottom of the jar.
2. **Add Chicken:** Layer grilled chicken breast on top of the rice.
3. **Add Vegetables:** Add cucumbers, cherry tomatoes, and olives.
4. **Add Cheese:** Sprinkle with crumbled feta cheese.
5. **Drizzle with Sauce:** Pour tzatziki sauce over the top.
6. **Store:** Refrigerate for up to 4 days. Shake or toss before serving.

Tips for Perfect Hearty Grain Bowls

- **Grain Preparation:** Cook grains in advance and allow them to cool before layering in jars. This prevents condensation and sogginess.
- **Layering:** Start with ingredients that can handle sitting in dressing or sauce, such as grains or proteins, and layer more delicate items like greens or cheese on top.
- **Dressing Storage:** Keep dressings separate until ready to eat to maintain the texture and freshness of your ingredients.
- **Portion Sizes:** Use appropriate jar sizes to ensure your ingredients fit well without overcrowding.

Nutritional Benefits

Hearty grain bowls provide a well-rounded meal with a balance of carbohydrates, proteins, and healthy fats. Grains offer sustained energy, while proteins and vegetables contribute essential nutrients and fiber. These bowls are perfect for a filling lunch or dinner that supports a healthy and active lifestyle.

Conclusion

Hearty grain bowls are an excellent way to create balanced, flavorful meals that are easy to prepare and store. With a variety of recipes to suit different tastes and dietary needs, these bowls offer a nutritious solution for busy days. Prepare them in advance and enjoy the convenience and satisfaction of a wholesome meal ready when you are.

Protein-Packed Jars 2.4.

Introduction

Protein-packed jars are a fantastic way to ensure you're getting the right amount of protein to fuel your day, support muscle growth, and keep you feeling full and satisfied. These jars are ideal for meal prepping, whether you need a quick lunch, a post-workout snack, or a balanced dinner. This chapter will walk you through the essentials of creating protein-packed jars, provide a variety of delicious recipes, and offer tips for maximizing flavor and nutrition.

Basic Protein-Packed Jar Preparation

Ingredients:

- Protein sources (such as cooked chicken, tofu, beans, lentils, or Greek yogurt)
- Vegetables (raw or cooked, including leafy greens, roasted veggies, or crunchy items)
- Carbohydrates (like grains, quinoa, or sweet potatoes)
- Dressings or sauces (to enhance flavor)
- Optional add-ins (cheese, nuts, seeds, or avocado)

Instructions:

1. **Layer Proteins:** Start with your primary protein source at the bottom of the jar to ensure it stays fresh.
2. **Add Carbohydrates:** Layer in your carbohydrate source next, such as cooked grains or sweet potatoes.
3. **Include Vegetables:** Add a variety of vegetables for nutrients and texture.
4. **Dress and Top:** Drizzle with dressing or sauce and finish with optional toppings.
5. **Store:** Seal the jar tightly and refrigerate. Protein-packed jars can generally be stored for up to 4 days.

Protein-Packed Jar Recipes

1. Grilled Chicken and Quinoa Jar

Ingredients:

- 1/2 cup cooked quinoa
- 1/2 cup grilled chicken breast, diced
- 1/4 cup cherry tomatoes, halved
- 1/4 cup diced cucumbers
- 1/4 cup shredded carrots
- 2 tablespoons balsamic vinaigrette

Instructions:

1. **Layer Quinoa:** Start with cooked quinoa at the bottom of the jar.
2. **Add Chicken:** Layer grilled chicken breast over the quinoa.
3. **Add Vegetables:** Add cherry tomatoes, cucumbers, and shredded carrots.
4. **Drizzle with Dressing:** Pour balsamic vinaigrette over the top.
5. **Store:** Refrigerate for up to 4 days. Shake before eating or serve with a spoon.

2. Spicy Tofu and Sweet Potato Jar

Ingredients:

- 1/2 cup roasted sweet potatoes
- 1/2 cup spicy tofu (cubed)
- 1/4 cup black beans
- 1/4 cup corn kernels
- 1/4 cup diced bell peppers
- 2 tablespoons lime-cilantro dressing

Instructions:

1. **Layer Sweet Potatoes:** Start with roasted sweet potatoes at the bottom.
2. **Add Tofu:** Layer spicy tofu over the sweet potatoes.
3. **Add Beans and Corn:** Add black beans and corn kernels.
4. **Add Peppers:** Add diced bell peppers.
5. **Drizzle with Dressing:** Pour lime-cilantro dressing over the top.
6. **Store:** Refrigerate for up to 4 days. Shake or toss before serving.

3. Lentil and Veggie Jar

Ingredients:

- 1/2 cup cooked lentils
- 1/4 cup diced roasted beets
- 1/4 cup chopped kale
- 1/4 cup shredded radishes
- 1/4 cup crumbled goat cheese
- 2 tablespoons tahini dressing

Instructions:

1. **Layer Lentils:** Start with cooked lentils at the bottom of the jar.
2. **Add Vegetables:** Layer roasted beets, chopped kale, and shredded radishes.
3. **Add Cheese:** Sprinkle with crumbled goat cheese.
4. **Drizzle with Dressing:** Pour tahini dressing over the top.
5. **Store:** Refrigerate for up to 4 days. Shake before eating or serve with a spoon.

4. Turkey and Brown Rice Jar

Ingredients:

- 1/2 cup cooked brown rice
- 1/2 cup ground turkey, cooked and seasoned
- 1/4 cup diced bell peppers
- 1/4 cup chopped spinach
- 1/4 cup cherry tomatoes, halved
- 2 tablespoons ranch dressing

Instructions:

1. **Layer Rice:** Start with cooked brown rice at the bottom.
2. **Add Turkey:** Layer ground turkey over the rice.
3. **Add Vegetables:** Add diced bell peppers, chopped spinach, and cherry tomatoes.
4. **Drizzle with Dressing:** Pour ranch dressing over the top.
5. **Store:** Refrigerate for up to 4 days. Shake before eating or enjoy cold.

5. Greek Yogurt and Chickpea Jar

Ingredients:

- 1/2 cup plain Greek yogurt
- 1/2 cup cooked chickpeas
- 1/4 cup diced cucumbers
- 1/4 cup cherry tomatoes, halved
- 1/4 cup kalamata olives
- 2 tablespoons tzatziki sauce

Instructions:

1. **Layer Yogurt:** Start with Greek yogurt at the bottom of the jar.
2. **Add Chickpeas:** Layer cooked chickpeas over the yogurt.
3. **Add Vegetables:** Add cucumbers, cherry tomatoes, and kalamata olives.
4. **Drizzle with Sauce:** Pour tzatziki sauce over the top.
5. **Store:** Refrigerate for up to 4 days. Stir before eating or serve with a spoon.

Tips for Perfect Protein-Packed Jars

- **Protein Preparation:** Cook and cool protein sources in advance to prevent them from releasing moisture into the jar.

- **Layering:** Always start with the ingredients that can handle being in contact with dressing, like grains or proteins, and layer more delicate ingredients on top.
- **Dressing Storage:** Keep dressings and sauces separate until ready to eat to maintain the texture of the other ingredients.
- **Portion Sizes:** Use jars that are appropriately sized for your portions to avoid overcrowding and ensure easy access to all ingredients.

Nutritional Benefits

Protein-packed jars offer a rich source of protein essential for muscle repair, immune function, and overall health. Combined with vegetables and healthy carbs, these jars provide a balanced and satisfying meal that supports energy levels and satiety.

Conclusion

Protein-packed jars are an excellent way to enjoy a nutritious and satisfying meal with minimal effort. With a variety of recipes to suit different tastes and dietary preferences, these jars offer a convenient solution for meal prepping and on-the-go eating. Prepare them in advance to ensure you have a delicious and protein-rich meal ready whenever you need it.

Vegetarian and Vegan Options 2.5.

Introduction

Vegetarian and vegan jars offer a fantastic way to enjoy plant-based meals that are not only nutritious but also delicious and satisfying. These jars are perfect for anyone looking to incorporate more plant-based meals into their diet, whether you're a committed vegetarian or vegan or simply looking to reduce your meat consumption. This chapter will guide you through creating flavorful vegetarian and vegan jars, provide a range of recipes, and offer tips for keeping your meals fresh and enjoyable.

Basic Vegetarian and Vegan Jar Preparation

Ingredients:

- Protein sources (such as beans, tofu, tempeh, or legumes)
- Vegetables (both raw and cooked, including leafy greens, roasted veggies, or crunchy items)
- Carbohydrates (like quinoa, brown rice, or sweet potatoes)
- Dressings or sauces (make sure they're plant-based)
- Optional add-ins (nuts, seeds, avocado, or nutritional yeast)

Instructions:

1. **Prepare Protein:** Start with your chosen plant-based protein source, ensuring it's cooke and cooled if necessary.
2. **Add Carbohydrates:** Layer in your carbohydrate source next, such as cooked grains or potatoes.
3. **Include Vegetables:** Add a variety of vegetables for nutrients and texture.
4. **Dress and Top:** Drizzle with a plant-based dressing or sauce and finish with optional toppings.
5. **Store:** Seal the jar tightly and refrigerate. Vegetarian and vegan jars can generally be stored for up to 4 days.

Vegetarian and Vegan Jar Recipes

1. Mediterranean Chickpea Jar

Ingredients:

- 1/2 cup cooked quinoa
- 1/2 cup chickpeas, rinsed and drained
- 1/4 cup diced cucumbers
- 1/4 cup cherry tomatoes, halved
- 1/4 cup kalamata olives
- 1/4 cup crumbled feta cheese (or vegan feta)
- 2 tablespoons tahini dressing

Instructions:

1. **Layer Quinoa:** Start with cooked quinoa at the bottom of the jar.
2. **Add Chickpeas:** Layer chickpeas over the quinoa.
3. **Add Vegetables:** Add cucumbers, cherry tomatoes, and kalamata olives.
4. **Add Cheese:** Sprinkle with crumbled feta or vegan feta.
5. **Drizzle with Dressing:** Pour tahini dressing over the top.
6. **Store:** Refrigerate for up to 4 days. Shake before eating or serve with a spoon.

2. Sweet Potato and Black Bean Jar

Ingredients:

- 1/2 cup roasted sweet potatoes
- 1/2 cup black beans, rinsed and drained
- 1/4 cup corn kernels
- 1/4 cup diced red bell peppers
- 1/4 cup diced avocado
- 2 tablespoons lime-cilantro dressing

Instructions:

1. **Layer Sweet Potatoes:** Start with roasted sweet potatoes at the bottom.
2. **Add Beans:** Layer black beans over the sweet potatoes.
3. **Add Corn and Peppers:** Add corn kernels and diced red bell peppers.
4. **Add Avocado:** Top with diced avocado.

5. **Drizzle with Dressing:** Pour lime-cilantro dressing over the top.
6. **Store:** Refrigerate for up to 4 days. Shake or toss before serving.

3. Vegan Lentil and Kale Jar

Ingredients:

- 1/2 cup cooked lentils
- 1/4 cup diced roasted beets
- 1/4 cup chopped kale
- 1/4 cup shredded carrots
- 2 tablespoons balsamic vinaigrette

Instructions:

1. **Layer Lentils:** Start with cooked lentils at the bottom of the jar.
2. **Add Vegetables:** Layer roasted beets, chopped kale, and shredded carrots.
3. **Drizzle with Dressing:** Pour balsamic vinaigrette over the top.
4. **Store:** Refrigerate for up to 4 days. Shake before eating or serve with a spoon.

4. Thai Peanut Tofu Jar

Ingredients:

- 1/2 cup cooked brown rice
- 1/2 cup tofu, cubed and pan-seared
- 1/4 cup shredded cabbage
- 1/4 cup julienned carrots
- 1/4 cup snap peas
- 2 tablespoons Thai peanut dressing

Instructions:

1. **Layer Rice:** Start with cooked brown rice at the bottom.
2. **Add Tofu:** Layer tofu over the rice.
3. **Add Vegetables:** Add shredded cabbage, julienned carrots, and snap peas.
4. **Drizzle with Dressing:** Pour Thai peanut dressing over the top.
5. **Store:** Refrigerate for up to 4 days. Shake or toss before serving.

5. Roasted Veggie and Hummus Jar

Ingredients:

- 1/2 cup roasted vegetables (such as bell peppers, zucchini, and eggplant)
- 1/2 cup cooked farro
- 1/4 cup hummus
- 1/4 cup diced cucumbers
- 1/4 cup cherry tomatoes, halved
- 2 tablespoons lemon-tahini dressing

Instructions:

1. **Layer Vegetables:** Start with roasted vegetables at the bottom.
2. **Add Farro:** Layer cooked farro over the vegetables.
3. **Add Hummus:** Add a dollop of hummus.
4. **Add Cucumbers and Tomatoes:** Add diced cucumbers and cherry tomatoes.
5. **Drizzle with Dressing:** Pour lemon-tahini dressing over the top.
6. **Store:** Refrigerate for up to 4 days. Stir before eating or serve with a spoon.

Tips for Perfect Vegetarian and Vegan Jars

- **Protein Preparation:** Use a variety of plant-based proteins to keep meals interesting and balanced. Ensure they are cooked and cooled before layering in the jars.
- **Layering:** Start with the denser ingredients, such as grains or roasted vegetables, and add more delicate items like greens or avocado on top.
- **Dressing Storage:** Keep dressings separate to avoid sogginess and to maintain the freshness of the vegetables and grains.
- **Portion Control:** Use appropriate jar sizes to ensure your ingredients fit well and to avoid overcrowding.

Nutritional Benefits

Vegetarian and vegan jars provide a rich source of essential nutrients from plant-based proteins, vitamins, minerals, and fiber. These meals support overall health, boost energy levels, and promote satiety without relying on animal products.

Conclusion

Vegetarian and vegan jars offer a diverse range of flavors and nutrients in a convenient and easy to-prepare format. Whether you're a long-time vegan or just looking to explore plant-based options, these jars provide delicious and satisfying meals that cater to a variety of tastes and dietary needs. Prepare them in advance to enjoy the benefits of nutritious, plant-based meals throughout the week.

International Flavors

Introduction

Exploring international flavors through meals in a jar allows you to enjoy a world of tastes and traditions right from your kitchen. From spicy Mexican bowls to tangy Thai salads, these recipes bring global cuisine to a convenient, portable format. This chapter will guide you through creating jars that feature bold, international flavors, offering a variety of recipes that cater to different tastes and dietary preferences. Whether you're craving something spicy, savory, or sweet, these international flavor jars will add a global twist to your meal prep routine.

Basic International Jar Preparation

Ingredients:

- Protein sources (such as chicken, tofu, beans, or legumes, adjusted to the specific cuisine)
- Carbohydrates (like rice, noodles, or grains, suitable for the flavor profile)
- Vegetables (raw or cooked, including traditional or complementary items from the cuisine)
- International sauces or dressings (to enhance flavor)
- Optional add-ins (herbs, nuts, seeds, or cheese, specific to the cuisine)

Instructions:

1. **Prepare Ingredients:** Cook and prepare protein, grains, and vegetables according to the recipe.
2. **Layer Proteins and Carbohydrates:** Start with your protein source at the bottom, followed by carbohydrates.
3. **Add Vegetables:** Layer vegetables that complement the cuisine's flavor profile.
4. **Dress and Top:** Drizzle with international sauces or dressings and finish with optional add-ins.
5. **Store:** Seal the jar tightly and refrigerate. These jars can generally be stored for up to 4 days.

International Flavor Jar Recipes

1. Mexican Burrito Bowl Jar

Ingredients:

- 1/2 cup cooked brown rice
- 1/2 cup black beans, rinsed and drained
- 1/4 cup corn kernels
- 1/4 cup diced red bell peppers
- 1/4 cup diced avocado
- 1/4 cup shredded cheddar cheese (or vegan cheese)
- 2 tablespoons salsa or chipotle dressing

Instructions:

1. **Layer Rice:** Start with cooked brown rice at the bottom of the jar.
2. **Add Beans and Corn:** Layer black beans and corn over the rice.
3. **Add Peppers and Avocado:** Add diced red bell peppers and avocado.
4. **Add Cheese:** Sprinkle with shredded cheddar cheese or vegan cheese.
5. **Drizzle with Salsa:** Pour salsa or chipotle dressing over the top.
6. **Store:** Refrigerate for up to 4 days. Shake before eating or serve with a spoon.

2. Thai Peanut Noodle Jar

Ingredients:

- 1/2 cup cooked rice noodles
- 1/2 cup tofu, cubed and pan-seared
- 1/4 cup shredded carrots
- 1/4 cup snap peas
- 1/4 cup chopped cilantro
- 2 tablespoons Thai peanut sauce

Instructions:

1. **Layer Noodles:** Start with cooked rice noodles at the bottom.
2. **Add Tofu:** Layer tofu over the noodles.
3. **Add Vegetables:** Add shredded carrots and snap peas.
4. **Add Cilantro:** Sprinkle with chopped cilantro.
5. **Drizzle with Sauce:** Pour Thai peanut sauce over the top.
6. **Store:** Refrigerate for up to 4 days. Shake or toss before serving.

3. Greek Mezze Jar

Ingredients:

- 1/2 cup cooked farro
- 1/4 cup hummus
- 1/4 cup diced cucumbers
- 1/4 cup cherry tomatoes, halved
- 1/4 cup kalamata olives
- 1/4 cup crumbled feta cheese (or vegan feta)
- 2 tablespoons tzatziki sauce

Instructions:

1. **Layer Farro:** Start with cooked farro at the bottom of the jar.
2. **Add Hummus:** Add a dollop of hummus on top of the farro.
3. **Add Vegetables:** Layer cucumbers, cherry tomatoes, and kalamata olives.
4. **Add Cheese:** Sprinkle with crumbled feta cheese or vegan feta.
5. **Drizzle with Sauce:** Pour tzatziki sauce over the top.
6. **Store:** Refrigerate for up to 4 days. Stir before eating or serve with a spoon.

4. Japanese Teriyaki Chicken Jar

Ingredients:

- 1/2 cup cooked jasmine rice
- 1/2 cup teriyaki chicken, diced
- 1/4 cup steamed broccoli
- 1/4 cup shredded carrots
- 1/4 cup edamame
- 2 tablespoons sesame ginger dressing

Instructions:

1. **Layer Rice:** Start with cooked jasmine rice at the bottom.
2. **Add Chicken:** Layer teriyaki chicken over the rice.

3. **Add Vegetables:** Add steamed broccoli, shredded carrots, and edamame.
4. **Drizzle with Dressing:** Pour sesame ginger dressing over the top.
5. **Store:** Refrigerate for up to 4 days. Shake or toss before serving.

5. Indian Chickpea Curry Jar

Ingredients:

- 1/2 cup cooked basmati rice
- 1/2 cup chickpea curry (prepared with spices like cumin, coriander, and turmeric)
- 1/4 cup diced cucumber
- 1/4 cup diced tomatoes
- 1/4 cup chopped cilantro
- 2 tablespoons raita or yogurt dressing (vegan if preferred)

Instructions:

1. **Layer Rice:** Start with cooked basmati rice at the bottom.
2. **Add Curry:** Layer chickpea curry over the rice.
3. **Add Vegetables:** Add diced cucumber and tomatoes.
4. **Add Cilantro:** Sprinkle with chopped cilantro.
5. **Drizzle with Raita:** Pour raita or yogurt dressing over the top.
6. **Store:** Refrigerate for up to 4 days. Stir before eating or serve with a spoon.

Tips for Perfect International Flavor Jars

- **Ingredient Preparation:** Prepare and cool proteins and grains before layering to prevent sogginess and ensure freshness.
- **Layering:** Begin with heavier or denser ingredients, such as grains or proteins, and layer more delicate items, like greens or herbs, on top.
- **Sauce Storage:** Keep sauces and dressings separate until ready to eat to maintain the texture of other ingredients.
- **Portion Control:** Use jars that fit the portion sizes of the recipes to ensure that the ingredients are well-distributed and easily accessible.

Nutritional Benefits

International flavor jars offer a diverse range of nutrients, from protein and fiber to vitamins and minerals. By incorporating global ingredients and flavors, these jars provide balanced meals that support overall health while introducing exciting new tastes and culinary traditions.

Conclusion

International flavor jars bring a world of cuisine into your meal prep routine, offering delicious and nutritious options that cater to various tastes and dietary needs. By experimenting with different global ingredients and recipes, you can enjoy a diverse range of flavors and maintain a healthy, balanced diet. Prepare these jars in advance to savor the tastes of international cuisine anytime you need a quick, satisfying meal.

Chapter 3:

Dinner Jars 3.1.

Introduction

Dinner jars offer a convenient and delicious way to enjoy a balanced meal without the hassle of cooking after a long day. These jars are perfect for meal prepping, allowing you to prepare hearty, nutritious dinners in advance. Whether you're looking for a quick weeknight dinner or a make-ahead option for busy evenings, dinner jars provide a solution that is both practical and flavorful. In this chapter, we'll explore various dinner jar recipes that cater to different tastes and dietary preferences, ensuring you have a delightful meal ready whenever you need it.

Basic Dinner Jar Preparation

Ingredients:

- Protein sources (such as chicken, beef, tofu, or beans)
- Carbohydrates (like rice, pasta, or potatoes)
- Vegetables (both raw and cooked, including hearty greens, roasted veggies, or crunchy items)
- Sauces or dressings (to enhance flavor)
- Optional add-ins (cheese, herbs, nuts, or seeds)

Instructions:

1. **Prepare Ingredients:** Cook and cool proteins, carbohydrates, and vegetables as needed
2. **Layer Proteins and Carbohydrates:** Start with your protein source at the bottom of the jar, followed by carbohydrates.
3. **Add Vegetables:** Layer vegetables on top of the carbohydrates.
4. **Dress and Top:** Drizzle with sauce or dressing and finish with optional add-ins.
5. **Store:** Seal the jar tightly and refrigerate. Dinner jars can generally be stored for up to 4 days.

Dinner Jar Recipes

1. Chicken and Veggie Stir-Fry Jar

Ingredients:

- 1/2 cup cooked brown rice
- 1/2 cup stir-fried chicken breast, sliced
- 1/4 cup snap peas
- 1/4 cup shredded carrots

- 1/4 cup red bell peppers, sliced
- 2 tablespoons teriyaki sauce

Instructions:

1. **Layer Rice:** Start with cooked brown rice at the bottom of the jar.
2. **Add Chicken:** Layer stir-fried chicken over the rice.
3. **Add Vegetables:** Add snap peas, shredded carrots, and red bell peppers.
4. **Drizzle with Sauce:** Pour teriyaki sauce over the top.
5. **Store:** Refrigerate for up to 4 days. Shake before eating or serve with a spoon.

2. Beef and Sweet Potato Jar

Ingredients:

- 1/2 cup cooked quinoa
- 1/2 cup ground beef, seasoned and cooked
- 1/2 cup roasted sweet potatoes
- 1/4 cup corn kernels
- 1/4 cup diced bell peppers
- 2 tablespoons chipotle sauce

Instructions:

1. **Layer Quinoa:** Start with cooked quinoa at the bottom.
2. **Add Beef:** Layer ground beef over the quinoa.
3. **Add Sweet Potatoes and Vegetables:** Add roasted sweet potatoes, corn kernels, and diced bell peppers.
4. **Drizzle with Sauce:** Pour chipotle sauce over the top.
5. **Store:** Refrigerate for up to 4 days. Shake or toss before serving.

3. Vegetarian Chili Jar

Ingredients:

- 1/2 cup cooked brown rice
- 1/2 cup vegetarian chili (prepared with beans, tomatoes, and spices)
- 1/4 cup shredded cheddar cheese (or vegan cheese)
- 1/4 cup diced avocado
- 2 tablespoons sour cream or vegan alternative

Instructions:

1. **Layer Rice:** Start with cooked brown rice at the bottom.
2. **Add Chili:** Layer vegetarian chili over the rice.
3. **Add Cheese:** Sprinkle with shredded cheddar cheese or vegan cheese.
4. **Add Avocado:** Top with diced avocado.
5. **Drizzle with Sour Cream:** Pour sour cream or vegan alternative over the top.
6. **Store:** Refrigerate for up to 4 days. Stir before eating or serve with a spoon.

4. Thai Curry Tofu Jar

Ingredients:

- 1/2 cup cooked jasmine rice
- 1/2 cup tofu, cubed and cooked in Thai curry sauce
- 1/4 cup steamed broccoli
- 1/4 cup diced bell peppers
- 1/4 cup snap peas
- 2 tablespoons coconut curry sauce

Instructions:

1. **Layer Rice:** Start with cooked jasmine rice at the bottom.
2. **Add Tofu:** Layer tofu over the rice.
3. **Add Vegetables:** Add steamed broccoli, diced bell peppers, and snap peas.
4. **Drizzle with Sauce:** Pour coconut curry sauce over the top.
5. **Store:** Refrigerate for up to 4 days. Shake or toss before serving.

5. Italian Pasta Jar

Ingredients:

- 1/2 cup cooked penne pasta
- 1/2 cup marinara sauce
- 1/4 cup cooked ground turkey or beef
- 1/4 cup diced zucchini
- 1/4 cup sliced black olives
- 2 tablespoons grated Parmesan cheese (or vegan cheese)

Instructions:

1. **Layer Pasta:** Start with cooked penne pasta at the bottom of the jar.
2. **Add Sauce:** Pour marinara sauce over the pasta.
3. **Add Meat and Vegetables:** Layer ground turkey or beef, diced zucchini, and sliced black olives.
4. **Add Cheese:** Sprinkle with grated Parmesan cheese or vegan cheese.
5. **Store:** Refrigerate for up to 4 days. Stir before eating or serve with a spoon.

Tips for Perfect Dinner Jars

- **Protein Preparation:** Cook proteins in advance and allow them to cool before layering to prevent them from releasing moisture into the jar.
- **Layering:** Start with ingredients that are less likely to get soggy, like grains or proteins and layer more delicate ingredients like greens or cheese on top.
- **Sauce Storage:** Keep sauces and dressings separate until ready to eat to maintain the texture of other ingredients.
- **Portion Control:** Use jars that are appropriately sized for your portions to ensure easy access and proper mixing of ingredients.

Nutritional Benefits

Dinner jars provide a balanced mix of protein, carbohydrates, and vegetables, offering essential nutrients that support energy levels and overall health. By incorporating a variety of ingredients and flavors, these jars make it easy to enjoy a nutritious meal that satisfies your cravings and dietary needs.

Conclusion

Dinner jars are a versatile and practical solution for enjoying hearty, delicious meals with minimal preparation. With a variety of recipes to suit different tastes and dietary preferences, these jars make it easy to have a satisfying dinner ready whenever you need it. Prepare them in advance to simplify your mealtime routine and enjoy the convenience of a homemade meal on demand.

Comfort Food Jars 3.2.

Introduction

Comfort food jars are all about indulgence and satisfaction, bringing warmth and coziness to your meals. These jars are perfect for those days when you crave hearty, familiar dishes that evoke a sense of home and nostalgia. From creamy mac and cheese to rich beef stew, comfort food jars are designed to offer the ultimate in taste and convenience. This chapter will guide you through creating comforting, delicious meals that you can prepare in advance and enjoy whenever you need a bit of culinary comfort.

Basic Comfort Food Jar Preparation

Ingredients:

- Protein sources (such as chicken, beef, sausage, or legumes)
- Carbohydrates (like pasta, rice, or potatoes)
- Vegetables (both cooked and raw, depending on the recipe)
- Rich sauces or gravies (to enhance flavor)
- Optional add-ins (cheese, herbs, or crispy toppings)

Instructions:

1. **Prepare Ingredients:** Cook and cool proteins, carbohydrates, and vegetables as needed.
2. **Layer Proteins and Carbohydrates:** Start with your protein source at the bottom of the jar, followed by carbohydrates.
3. **Add Vegetables:** Layer vegetables on top of the carbohydrates.
4. **Add Sauces:** Pour or spoon rich sauces or gravies over the top.
5. **Store:** Seal the jar tightly and refrigerate. Comfort food jars can generally be stored for up to 4 days.

Comfort Food Jar Recipes

1. Classic Mac and Cheese Jar

Ingredients:

- 1/2 cup cooked elbow macaroni
- 1/2 cup creamy cheddar cheese sauce
- 1/4 cup cooked and crumbled bacon (optional)
- 1/4 cup frozen peas (thawed)
- 2 tablespoons breadcrumbs (for topping)

Instructions:

1. **Layer Macaroni:** Start with cooked elbow macaroni at the bottom of the jar.
2. **Add Cheese Sauce:** Pour creamy cheddar cheese sauce over the macaroni.
3. **Add Bacon and Peas:** Add crumbled bacon and thawed peas.
4. **Add Breadcrumbs:** Sprinkle with breadcrumbs.
5. **Store:** Refrigerate for up to 4 days. Reheat thoroughly before serving.

2. Beef Stroganoff Jar

Ingredients:

- 1/2 cup cooked egg noodles
- 1/2 cup beef stroganoff (prepared with tender beef strips, mushrooms, and a creamy sauce)
- 1/4 cup steamed green beans
- 1 tablespoon chopped fresh parsley (for garnish)

Instructions:

1. **Layer Noodles:** Start with cooked egg noodles at the bottom of the jar.
2. **Add Beef Stroganoff:** Layer beef stroganoff over the noodles.
3. **Add Green Beans:** Add steamed green beans on top.
4. **Garnish:** Sprinkle with chopped parsley.
5. **Store:** Refrigerate for up to 4 days. Reheat thoroughly before serving.

3. Chicken Pot Pie Jar

Ingredients:

- 1/2 cup cooked diced chicken
- 1/4 cup frozen mixed vegetables (carrots, peas, corn)
- 1/4 cup creamy pot pie filling (prepared with a roux and chicken broth)
- 1/4 cup biscuit dough (store-bought or homemade)

Instructions:

1. **Layer Chicken:** Start with cooked diced chicken at the bottom of the jar.
2. **Add Vegetables:** Layer frozen mixed vegetables over the chicken.
3. **Add Pot Pie Filling:** Pour creamy pot pie filling over the vegetables.

4. **Top with Biscuit Dough:** Drop biscuit dough over the filling.
5. **Store:** Refrigerate for up to 4 days. Bake in an oven-safe dish until biscuit dough is cooked through and golden.

4. Shepherd's Pie Jar

Ingredients:

- 1/2 cup cooked ground beef or lamb
- 1/4 cup cooked peas and carrots
- 1/4 cup creamy mashed potatoes
- 1 tablespoon shredded cheddar cheese

Instructions:

1. **Layer Meat:** Start with cooked ground beef or lamb at the bottom of the jar.
2. **Add Vegetables:** Layer cooked peas and carrots over the meat.
3. **Top with Mashed Potatoes:** Spread creamy mashed potatoes on top.
4. **Add Cheese:** Sprinkle with shredded cheddar cheese.
5. **Store:** Refrigerate for up to 4 days. Reheat thoroughly before serving.

5. Creamy Tomato Soup Jar

Ingredients:

- 1/2 cup creamy tomato soup (prepared with tomatoes, cream, and herbs)
- 1/4 cup cooked pasta (like penne or macaroni)
- 1/4 cup shredded mozzarella cheese
- 2 tablespoons croutons

Instructions:

1. **Layer Soup:** Start with creamy tomato soup at the bottom of the jar.
2. **Add Pasta:** Add cooked pasta over the soup.
3. **Add Cheese:** Sprinkle with shredded mozzarella cheese.
4. **Top with Croutons:** Add croutons on top.
5. **Store:** Refrigerate for up to 4 days. Reheat thoroughly before serving.

Tips for Perfect Comfort Food Jars

- **Ingredient Preparation:** Ensure all ingredients are cooked and cooled before layering to prevent sogginess and maintain texture.
- **Layering:** Start with denser ingredients like proteins and carbohydrates at the bottom, and layer more delicate ingredients like cheese or toppings on top.
- **Sauce Storage:** To avoid sogginess, consider keeping rich sauces or gravies separate until ready to eat.
- **Portion Control:** Use jars that are appropriately sized for your portions to ensure even mixing and easy serving.

Nutritional Benefits

Comfort food jars offer a comforting balance of flavors and nutrients, providing a satisfying meal that can be both indulgent and nourishing. By incorporating a variety of proteins, carbohydrates, and vegetables, these jars deliver essential nutrients while keeping your taste buds happy.

Conclusion

Comfort food jars bring a touch of warmth and familiarity to your meal prep routine, offering hearty, satisfying options that are perfect for busy days or when you need a bit of culinary comfort. With a range of recipes to suit different tastes and dietary needs, these jars make it easy to enjoy your favorite comfort foods any time you want.

Low-Carb and Keto Options 3.3.

Introduction

Low-carb and keto diets focus on reducing carbohydrate intake to encourage the body to burn fat for energy. Meals in a jar can easily accommodate these dietary preferences by incorporating high-protein, high-fat ingredients while minimizing carbohydrates. This chapter explores delicious and satisfying low-carb and keto-friendly jar recipes that are both convenient and nutritious. Perfect for anyone following a low-carb lifestyle or simply looking to reduce their carb intake, these jars offer a variety of flavors and textures while staying within your dietary goals.

Basic Low-Carb and Keto Jar Preparation

Ingredients:

- Protein sources (such as chicken, beef, tofu, or eggs)
- Low-carb vegetables (like leafy greens, broccoli, or cauliflower)
- Healthy fats (such as avocado, cheese, or nuts)
- Low-carb sauces or dressings (to enhance flavor)
- Optional add-ins (seeds, herbs, or keto-friendly condiments)

Instructions:

1. **Prepare Ingredients:** Cook and cool proteins, and prepare low-carb vegetables and other add-ins as needed.
2. **Layer Proteins and Vegetables:** Start with your protein source at the bottom of the jar, followed by vegetables.
3. **Add Fats:** Incorporate healthy fats like avocado or cheese.
4. **Dress and Top:** Drizzle with low-carb sauces or dressings and finish with optional add-ins.

5. **Store:** Seal the jar tightly and refrigerate. These jars can generally be stored for up to 4 days.

Low-Carb and Keto Jar Recipes

1. Chicken Caesar Salad Jar

Ingredients:

- 1/2 cup cooked, diced chicken breast
- 1 cup chopped romaine lettuce
- 1/4 cup grated Parmesan cheese
- 1/4 cup sliced black olives
- 2 tablespoons Caesar dressing (low-carb)

Instructions:

1. **Layer Chicken:** Start with cooked, diced chicken breast at the bottom of the jar.
2. **Add Lettuce:** Layer chopped romaine lettuce over the chicken.
3. **Add Cheese and Olives:** Sprinkle with grated Parmesan cheese and add sliced black olives.
4. **Drizzle with Dressing:** Pour Caesar dressing over the top.
5. **Store:** Refrigerate for up to 4 days. Shake before eating or serve with a fork.

2. Beef and Broccoli Stir-Fry Jar

Ingredients:

- 1/2 cup cooked sliced beef (such as flank steak or sirloin)
- 1/2 cup steamed broccoli florets
- 1/4 cup sliced bell peppers
- 2 tablespoons soy sauce (or tamari for gluten-free)
- 1 tablespoon sesame oil

Instructions:

1. **Layer Beef:** Start with cooked sliced beef at the bottom of the jar.
2. **Add Vegetables:** Layer steamed broccoli and sliced bell peppers over the beef.
3. **Add Sauce:** Drizzle with soy sauce and sesame oil.
4. **Store:** Refrigerate for up to 4 days. Shake or toss before serving.

3. Avocado and Egg Salad Jar

Ingredients:

- 1/2 cup chopped hard-boiled eggs
- 1/2 avocado, diced
- 1/4 cup diced celery
- 2 tablespoons mayonnaise (keto-friendly)
- 1 tablespoon chopped chives

Instructions:

1. **Layer Eggs:** Start with chopped hard-boiled eggs at the bottom of the jar.
2. **Add Avocado:** Add diced avocado on top of the eggs.
3. **Add Celery:** Layer diced celery over the avocado.
4. **Add Mayonnaise and Chives:** Stir in mayonnaise and sprinkle with chopped chives.
5. **Store:** Refrigerate for up to 4 days. Stir before eating.

4. Salmon and Spinach Jar

Ingredients:

- 1/2 cup cooked, flaked salmon
- 1 cup fresh spinach
- 1/4 cup diced cucumber
- 2 tablespoons dill sauce (keto-friendly)

Instructions:

1. **Layer Salmon:** Start with cooked, flaked salmon at the bottom of the jar.
2. **Add Spinach:** Layer fresh spinach over the salmon.
3. **Add Cucumber:** Add diced cucumber on top of the spinach.
4. **Drizzle with Sauce:** Pour dill sauce over the top.
5. **Store:** Refrigerate for up to 4 days. Shake or toss before serving.

5. Zucchini Noodles with Pesto Jar

Ingredients:

- 1/2 cup spiralized zucchini noodles (zoodles)
- 1/4 cup cherry tomatoes, halved
- 1/4 cup shredded mozzarella cheese
- 2 tablespoons basil pesto (keto-friendly)

Instructions:

1. **Layer Zoodles:** Start with spiralized zucchini noodles at the bottom of the jar.
2. **Add Tomatoes:** Layer cherry tomatoes over the zoodles.
3. **Add Cheese:** Sprinkle with shredded mozzarella cheese.
4. **Drizzle with Pesto:** Pour basil pesto over the top.
5. **Store:** Refrigerate for up to 4 days. Stir before eating or serve with a fork.

Tips for Perfect Low-Carb and Keto Jars

- **Ingredient Preparation:** Ensure proteins are cooked and cooled, and vegetables are prepared to maintain freshness and prevent sogginess.
- **Layering:** Start with proteins and vegetables at the bottom, and add cheese or fats on top to avoid mixing until ready to eat.
- **Sauce Storage:** Keep sauces or dressings separate until ready to eat to preserve the texture of other ingredients.

- **Portion Control:** Use appropriately sized jars to ensure that portions are manageable and ingredients are well-distributed.

Nutritional Benefits

Low-carb and keto jars are designed to provide high-quality proteins, healthy fats, and essential nutrients while minimizing carbohydrate content. These jars support sustained energy levels and contribute to overall health, while adhering to low-carb or ketogenic dietary guidelines.

Conclusion

Low-carb and keto jars offer a flavorful and convenient way to stick to your dietary goals without sacrificing taste or satisfaction. With a variety of recipes that cater to different preferences and needs, these jars make it easy to enjoy delicious, low-carb meals any time you need them. Prepare these jars in advance to streamline your meal prep and enjoy the benefits of a well-balanced, low-carb diet.

One-Pot Meals 3.4.

Introduction

One-pot meals are the epitome of convenience and flavor, allowing you to prepare a complete meal with minimal cleanup. These meals combine proteins, vegetables, and carbohydrates into a single dish, making them ideal for busy weeknights or meal prepping. In this chapter, we'll explore a range of one-pot meal jar recipes that offer hearty, satisfying options for any palate. These recipes are designed to be assembled in jars, making them easy to store, transport, and enjoy.

Basic One-Pot Meal Jar Preparation

Ingredients:

- Proteins (such as chicken, beef, seafood, or legumes)
- Carbohydrates (like rice, pasta, or quinoa)
- Vegetables (both fresh and cooked)
- Flavorful liquids (broth, sauce, or seasoning blends)
- Optional add-ins (cheese, herbs, or crunchy toppings)

Instructions:

1. **Prepare Ingredients:** Cook and cool proteins, and prepare vegetables and carbohydrates as needed.
2. **Layer Proteins and Carbohydrates:** Start with proteins at the bottom of the jar, followed by carbohydrates.
3. **Add Vegetables:** Layer vegetables on top of the carbohydrates.

4. **Add Liquid:** Pour flavorful liquids over the top.
5. **Store:** Seal the jar tightly and refrigerate. One-pot meal jars can generally be stored for up to 4 days.

One-Pot Meal Jar Recipes

1. Chicken and Rice Soup Jar

Ingredients:

- 1/2 cup cooked shredded chicken
- 1/2 cup cooked brown rice
- 1/2 cup diced carrots
- 1/4 cup chopped celery
- 1/4 cup frozen peas
- 1 cup chicken broth
- 1/2 teaspoon dried thyme

Instructions:

1. **Layer Chicken:** Start with cooked shredded chicken at the bottom of the jar.
2. **Add Rice:** Layer cooked brown rice over the chicken.
3. **Add Vegetables:** Add diced carrots, chopped celery, and frozen peas.
4. **Add Broth and Seasoning:** Pour chicken broth over the top and sprinkle with dried thyme.
5. **Store:** Refrigerate for up to 4 days. Reheat thoroughly before serving.

2. Beef and Vegetable Stew Jar

Ingredients:

- 1/2 cup cooked beef stew meat (cubed)
- 1/2 cup diced potatoes
- 1/2 cup chopped onions
- 1/2 cup chopped carrots
- 1/4 cup green beans
- 1 cup beef broth
- 1 tablespoon tomato paste

Instructions:

1. **Layer Beef:** Start with cooked beef stew meat at the bottom of the jar.
2. **Add Vegetables:** Layer diced potatoes, chopped onions, chopped carrots, and green beans over the beef.
3. **Add Broth and Tomato Paste:** Mix beef broth and tomato paste, then pour over the top
4. **Store:** Refrigerate for up to 4 days. Reheat thoroughly before serving.

3. Vegetarian Chili Jar

Ingredients:

- 1/2 cup cooked kidney beans
- 1/2 cup cooked black beans
- 1/2 cup diced tomatoes
- 1/2 cup corn kernels
- 1/4 cup chopped bell peppers
- 1 tablespoon chili powder
- 1 cup vegetable broth

Instructions:

1. **Layer Beans:** Start with cooked kidney beans and black beans at the bottom of the jar.
2. **Add Vegetables:** Layer diced tomatoes, corn kernels, and chopped bell peppers over the beans.
3. **Add Seasoning and Broth:** Sprinkle chili powder and pour vegetable broth over the top.
4. **Store:** Refrigerate for up to 4 days. Reheat thoroughly before serving.

4. Shrimp and Quinoa Bowl Jar

Ingredients:

- 1/2 cup cooked quinoa
- 1/2 cup cooked shrimp (peeled and deveined)
- 1/4 cup diced cucumbers
- 1/4 cup cherry tomatoes, halved
- 2 tablespoons tzatziki sauce

Instructions:

1. **Layer Quinoa:** Start with cooked quinoa at the bottom of the jar.
2. **Add Shrimp:** Layer cooked shrimp over the quinoa.
3. **Add Vegetables:** Add diced cucumbers and cherry tomatoes.
4. **Drizzle with Sauce:** Pour tzatziki sauce over the top.
5. **Store:** Refrigerate for up to 4 days. Stir before serving.

5. Sausage and Pepper Pasta Jar

Ingredients:

- 1/2 cup cooked penne pasta
- 1/2 cup cooked sausage slices
- 1/4 cup sliced bell peppers
- 1/4 cup chopped onions
- 1/4 cup marinara sauce
- 1/4 cup shredded mozzarella cheese

Instructions:

1. **Layer Pasta:** Start with cooked penne pasta at the bottom of the jar.
2. **Add Sausage and Vegetables:** Layer cooked sausage slices, sliced bell peppers, and chopped onions over the pasta.
3. **Add Sauce:** Pour marinara sauce over the top.
4. **Top with Cheese:** Sprinkle with shredded mozzarella cheese.

5. **Store:** Refrigerate for up to 4 days. Reheat thoroughly before serving.

Tips for Perfect One-Pot Meal Jars

- **Ingredient Preparation:** Cook proteins and carbohydrates thoroughly before layering. Ensure vegetables are cut to appropriate sizes to cook evenly.
- **Layering:** Start with ingredients that can handle longer cooking times, such as proteins and grains, and layer more delicate ingredients on top.
- **Liquid Measurement:** Ensure you use the right amount of liquid to prevent the ingredients from drying out or becoming too soggy.
- **Portion Control:** Use jars that are appropriately sized for your portions to maintain easy serving and mixing.

Nutritional Benefits

One-pot meals are a great way to enjoy a balanced diet, combining proteins, vegetables, and carbohydrates in a single dish. These meals are nutrient-dense and can be tailored to meet various dietary needs, providing essential vitamins and minerals while maintaining convenience

Conclusion

One-pot meal jars simplify your meal prep and offer a convenient solution for enjoying complete, flavorful meals with minimal cleanup. By preparing these meals in advance, you can ensure that you always have a satisfying and nutritious option ready to go. With a range of recipes to suit different tastes and dietary preferences, these jars make it easy to enjoy delicious hearty meals anytime.

Family Favorites 3.5.

Introduction

Family favorite meals are all about comfort, nostalgia, and creating shared moments around the table. Whether it's a classic casserole, a beloved pasta dish, or a hearty stew, these recipes bring a sense of warmth and togetherness to mealtime. In this chapter, we'll explore how to transform classic family favorites into convenient jar-friendly meals. These recipes are designed to appeal to all ages, making them perfect for family dinners, meal prepping, or potluck gatherings. Enjoy the ease of having beloved dishes ready to go, without compromising on taste or quality.

Basic Family Favorites Jar Preparation

Ingredients:

- Proteins (such as chicken, beef, or beans)

- Carbohydrates (like pasta, rice, or potatoes)
- Vegetables (both cooked and fresh)
- Flavorful sauces or gravies
- Optional add-ins (cheese, herbs, or crispy toppings)

Instructions:

1. **Prepare Ingredients:** Cook and cool proteins, and prepare vegetables and carbohydrates as needed.
2. **Layer Proteins and Carbohydrates:** Start with your protein source at the bottom of the jar, followed by carbohydrates.
3. **Add Vegetables:** Layer vegetables on top of the carbohydrates.
4. **Add Sauce or Gravy:** Pour or spoon sauces or gravies over the top.
5. **Store:** Seal the jar tightly and refrigerate. These jars can generally be stored for up to 4 days.

Family Favorite Jar Recipes

1. Classic Meatloaf Jar

Ingredients:

- 1/2 cup cooked and crumbled meatloaf
- 1/2 cup mashed potatoes
- 1/4 cup steamed green beans
- 2 tablespoons meatloaf sauce (ketchup or BBQ sauce)

Instructions:

1. **Layer Meatloaf:** Start with cooked and crumbled meatloaf at the bottom of the jar.
2. **Add Mashed Potatoes:** Layer mashed potatoes over the meatloaf.
3. **Add Vegetables:** Add steamed green beans on top.
4. **Drizzle with Sauce:** Spoon meatloaf sauce over the top.
5. **Store:** Refrigerate for up to 4 days. Reheat thoroughly before serving.

2. Creamy Chicken Alfredo Jar

Ingredients:

- 1/2 cup cooked fettuccine pasta
- 1/2 cup cooked diced chicken breast
- 1/4 cup steamed broccoli
- 1/4 cup Alfredo sauce
- 2 tablespoons grated Parmesan cheese

Instructions:

1. **Layer Pasta:** Start with cooked fettuccine pasta at the bottom of the jar.
2. **Add Chicken:** Layer cooked diced chicken breast over the pasta.
3. **Add Vegetables:** Add steamed broccoli on top of the chicken.

4. **Add Sauce and Cheese:** Pour Alfredo sauce over the top and sprinkle with grated Parmesan cheese.
5. **Store:** Refrigerate for up to 4 days. Reheat thoroughly before serving.

3. Taco Night Jar

Ingredients:

- 1/2 cup seasoned ground beef
- 1/4 cup black beans
- 1/4 cup corn kernels
- 1/4 cup shredded lettuce
- 2 tablespoons salsa
- 2 tablespoons shredded cheddar cheese

Instructions:

1. **Layer Beef:** Start with seasoned ground beef at the bottom of the jar.
2. **Add Beans and Corn:** Layer black beans and corn kernels over the beef.
3. **Add Lettuce:** Add shredded lettuce on top.
4. **Drizzle with Salsa and Cheese:** Spoon salsa over the top and sprinkle with shredded cheddar cheese.
5. **Store:** Refrigerate for up to 4 days. Stir before eating or serve with tortilla chips.

4. Spaghetti and Meatballs Jar

Ingredients:

- 1/2 cup cooked spaghetti
- 2-3 cooked meatballs
- 1/2 cup marinara sauce
- 2 tablespoons grated Parmesan cheese

Instructions:

1. **Layer Spaghetti:** Start with cooked spaghetti at the bottom of the jar.
2. **Add Meatballs:** Place cooked meatballs on top of the spaghetti.
3. **Add Sauce:** Pour marinara sauce over the meatballs.
4. **Top with Cheese:** Sprinkle with grated Parmesan cheese.
5. **Store:** Refrigerate for up to 4 days. Reheat thoroughly before serving.

5. Cheesy Broccoli and Rice Casserole Jar

Ingredients:

- 1/2 cup cooked rice
- 1/2 cup steamed broccoli florets
- 1/2 cup shredded cheddar cheese
- 1/4 cup creamy cheese sauce

Instructions:

1. **Layer Rice:** Start with cooked rice at the bottom of the jar.
2. **Add Broccoli:** Layer steamed broccoli over the rice.
3. **Add Cheese and Sauce:** Sprinkle with shredded cheddar cheese and pour creamy cheese sauce on top.
4. **Store:** Refrigerate for up to 4 days. Reheat thoroughly before serving.

Tips for Perfect Family Favorite Jars

- **Ingredient Preparation:** Ensure that all ingredients are cooked and cooled before layering to prevent sogginess and preserve texture.
- **Layering:** Start with hearty ingredients at the bottom and layer more delicate items on top to maintain freshness.
- **Sauce Storage:** To avoid sogginess, consider keeping sauces or gravies separate until ready to eat.
- **Portion Control:** Use jars of appropriate sizes to maintain proper portioning and ensure even mixing.

Nutritional Benefits

Family favorite jars offer a balanced combination of proteins, carbohydrates, and vegetables, making them both satisfying and nutritious. These jars can be adapted to include healthier ingredients while still retaining the comforting flavors that make them family favorites.

Conclusion

Family favorite jars combine the convenience of meal prepping with the comforting tastes that bring families together. By preparing these beloved dishes in jar form, you can enjoy easy, delicious meals that cater to everyone's tastes and dietary needs. With a variety of recipes to choose from, these jars make it simple to have a comforting, home-cooked meal ready whenever you need it.

Gourmet in a Jar

Introduction

Gourmet meals are often associated with elaborate preparations and fine dining experiences, but they can also be enjoyed in a convenient and portable form. Gourmet in a jar combines the elegance of high-end cuisine with the practicality of meal prep. This chapter features recipes that offer refined flavors and sophisticated ingredients, all beautifully layered and ready to enjoy. Whether you're preparing for a special occasion or simply want to elevate your everyday meals, these gourmet jars provide a touch of luxury with minimal effort.

Basic Gourmet Jar Preparation

Ingredients:

- High-quality proteins (such as seafood, tender cuts of meat, or artisanal cheeses)
- Specialty vegetables (like roasted heirloom tomatoes, wild mushrooms, or microgreens)
- Gourmet carbohydrates (such as truffle-infused rice, quinoa, or hand-cut pasta)
- Exquisite sauces or dressings (like balsamic reduction, beurre blanc, or saffron aioli)
- Optional garnishes (herbs, edible flowers, or premium nuts)

Instructions:

1. **Prepare Ingredients:** Cook and cool proteins and carbohydrates. Prepare vegetables and sauces according to recipe instructions.
2. **Layer Ingredients:** Start with the base ingredients (proteins or carbohydrates) at the bottom of the jar. Add vegetables and sauces in layers.
3. **Add Sauces and Garnishes:** Drizzle with sauces or dressings and add any garnishes on top.
4. **Store:** Seal the jar tightly and refrigerate. Gourmet jars are typically good for up to 4 days.

Gourmet Jar Recipes

1. Lobster and Truffle Risotto Jar

Ingredients:

- 1/2 cup cooked truffle risotto
- 1/4 cup cooked lobster meat
- 2 tablespoons sautéed wild mushrooms
- 2 tablespoons grated Parmesan cheese
- 1 teaspoon truffle oil

Instructions:

1. **Layer Risotto:** Start with cooked truffle risotto at the bottom of the jar.
2. **Add Lobster:** Layer cooked lobster meat over the risotto.
3. **Add Mushrooms:** Add sautéed wild mushrooms on top of the lobster.
4. **Drizzle with Oil and Cheese:** Drizzle with truffle oil and sprinkle with grated Parmesan cheese.
5. **Store:** Refrigerate for up to 4 days. Reheat thoroughly before serving.

2. Duck Confit and Red Cabbage Jar

Ingredients:

- 1/2 cup shredded duck confit
- 1/2 cup braised red cabbage
- 1/4 cup roasted baby potatoes
- 2 tablespoons port wine reduction

Instructions:

1. **Layer Duck Confit:** Start with shredded duck confit at the bottom of the jar.
2. **Add Cabbage:** Layer braised red cabbage over the duck.
3. **Add Potatoes:** Add roasted baby potatoes on top of the cabbage.
4. **Drizzle with Reduction:** Pour port wine reduction over the top.
5. **Store:** Refrigerate for up to 4 days. Reheat thoroughly before serving.

3. Salmon and Asparagus with Hollandaise Sauce Jar

Ingredients:

- 1/2 cup cooked salmon fillet, flaked
- 1/2 cup steamed asparagus tips
- 1/4 cup cooked quinoa
- 2 tablespoons hollandaise sauce
- 1 teaspoon fresh dill

Instructions:

1. **Layer Quinoa:** Start with cooked quinoa at the bottom of the jar.
2. **Add Salmon:** Layer flaked salmon fillet over the quinoa.
3. **Add Asparagus:** Add steamed asparagus tips on top of the salmon.
4. **Drizzle with Sauce:** Pour hollandaise sauce over the asparagus and sprinkle with fresh dill.
5. **Store:** Refrigerate for up to 4 days. Reheat thoroughly before serving.

4. Fig and Goat Cheese Salad Jar

Ingredients:

- 1/2 cup mixed baby greens
- 1/4 cup crumbled goat cheese
- 1/4 cup sliced fresh figs
- 2 tablespoons candied pecans
- 2 tablespoons balsamic vinaigrette

Instructions:

1. **Layer Greens:** Start with mixed baby greens at the bottom of the jar.
2. **Add Cheese and Figs:** Layer crumbled goat cheese and sliced fresh figs over the greens.
3. **Add Pecans:** Sprinkle with candied pecans.
4. **Drizzle with Vinaigrette:** Pour balsamic vinaigrette over the top.
5. **Store:** Refrigerate for up to 4 days. Toss before serving.

5. Beef Wellington Jar

Ingredients:

- 1/2 cup cooked beef tenderloin, sliced
- 1/4 cup mushroom duxelles
- 1/4 cup puff pastry pieces (pre-baked)

- 2 tablespoons red wine jus

Instructions:

1. **Layer Beef:** Start with sliced beef tenderloin at the bottom of the jar.
2. **Add Duxelles:** Layer mushroom duxelles over the beef.
3. **Add Pastry Pieces:** Add puff pastry pieces on top of the duxelles.
4. **Drizzle with Jus:** Pour red wine jus over the top.
5. **Store:** Refrigerate for up to 4 days. Reheat thoroughly before serving.

Tips for Perfect Gourmet Jars

- **Ingredient Quality:** Use high-quality, fresh ingredients to achieve the best flavor and presentation.
- **Layering:** Start with heavier ingredients at the bottom and layer more delicate items on top to maintain texture and flavor.
- **Sauce Application:** Keep sauces or dressings separate until ready to eat to prevent sogginess.
- **Garnishing:** Add garnishes just before serving to maintain their freshness and visual appeal.

Nutritional Benefits

Gourmet jars can be both indulgent and balanced, offering a variety of proteins, vegetables, and healthy fats. By using premium ingredients and carefully crafted sauces, these jars provide a luxurious dining experience that is also nourishing.

Conclusion

Gourmet in a jar brings the sophistication of fine dining to the convenience of meal prep. These recipes offer a range of refined flavors and elegant presentations, making it easy to enjoy high-end cuisine anytime. Whether for a special occasion or a regular treat, these gourmet jars provide a touch of luxury with the practicality of everyday meals.

Chapter 4:

Snack Jars 4.1.

Introduction

Snacks are an essential part of our daily routine, offering a quick energy boost and satisfying our cravings between meals. Snack jars provide a convenient and portable way to enjoy healthy, delicious snacks on the go. This chapter features a variety of snack jar recipes that cater to different tastes and dietary preferences, from crunchy and savory to sweet and satisfying. Whether you're prepping for a busy workday or looking for an easy after-school treat, these snack jars are designed to be both nutritious and enjoyable.

Basic Snack Jar Preparation

Ingredients:

- Fresh fruits and vegetables
- Protein-rich foods (like nuts, cheese, or yogurt)
- Whole grains (such as granola, crackers, or popcorn)
- Dips and spreads (like hummus, guacamole, or nut butters)
- Sweet treats (like dried fruits or dark chocolate)

Instructions:

1. **Prepare Ingredients:** Wash, chop, and portion fruits, vegetables, and other ingredients. Prepare dips and spreads as needed.
2. **Layer Ingredients:** Start with ingredients that may release moisture or become soggy, such as dips, at the bottom of the jar.
3. **Add Protein and Grains:** Layer protein-rich foods and whole grains on top of the dips.
4. **Add Fresh Produce:** Place fresh fruits and vegetables on the top to maintain their crispness.
5. **Store:** Seal the jar tightly and refrigerate. Snack jars can typically be stored for up to 3 days.

Snack Jar Recipes

1. Veggie and Hummus Jar

Ingredients:

- 1/4 cup hummus
- 1/2 cup sliced cucumbers
- 1/2 cup cherry tomatoes
- 1/4 cup sliced bell peppers
- 1/4 cup baby carrots

Instructions:

1. **Layer Hummus:** Start with hummus at the bottom of the jar.
2. **Add Vegetables:** Layer sliced cucumbers, cherry tomatoes, sliced bell peppers, and baby carrots over the hummus.
3. **Store:** Refrigerate for up to 3 days. Enjoy with a spoon or dip the vegetables into the hummus.

2. Fruit and Yogurt Parfait Jar

Ingredients:

- 1/2 cup Greek yogurt
- 1/4 cup granola
- 1/4 cup mixed berries (blueberries, raspberries, strawberries)
- 1 tablespoon honey

Instructions:

1. **Layer Yogurt:** Start with Greek yogurt at the bottom of the jar.
2. **Add Granola:** Layer granola over the yogurt.
3. **Add Berries:** Top with mixed berries.
4. **Drizzle with Honey:** Drizzle honey over the top.
5. **Store:** Refrigerate for up to 3 days. Stir before eating if desired.

3. Cheese and Crackers Jar

Ingredients:

- 1/4 cup cubed cheddar cheese
- 1/4 cup cubed gouda cheese
- 1/2 cup whole grain crackers
- 1/4 cup sliced apples

Instructions:

1. **Layer Cheese:** Start with cubed cheddar and gouda cheese at the bottom of the jar.
2. **Add Crackers:** Layer whole grain crackers over the cheese.
3. **Add Apples:** Place sliced apples on top of the crackers.
4. **Store:** Refrigerate for up to 3 days. Enjoy as a portable snack.

4. Nut and Dried Fruit Mix Jar

Ingredients:

- 1/4 cup almonds
- 1/4 cup walnuts
- 1/4 cup dried cranberries
- 1/4 cup dried apricots, chopped

Instructions:

1. **Layer Nuts and Fruit:** Start by layering almonds, walnuts, dried cranberries, and dried apricots in the jar.
2. **Store:** Seal the jar tightly. This snack can be stored at room temperature for up to 1 week or refrigerated for longer freshness.

5. Apple Slices with Peanut Butter Jar

Ingredients:

- 1/2 cup apple slices
- 1/4 cup peanut butter (or almond butter)
- 1 tablespoon raisins

Instructions:

1. **Layer Peanut Butter:** Start with peanut butter at the bottom of the jar.
2. **Add Apple Slices:** Place apple slices on top of the peanut butter.
3. **Add Raisins:** Sprinkle raisins over the apple slices.
4. **Store:** Refrigerate for up to 3 days. Stir the peanut butter if it separates before serving.

Tips for Perfect Snack Jars

- **Ingredient Preparation:** Ensure all ingredients are fresh and properly prepped to maintain taste and texture.
- **Layering:** Start with items that are less likely to become soggy at the bottom of the jar, such as dips and spreads, and add fresh produce on top.
- **Portion Control:** Use jars of appropriate sizes to manage portion control and keep snacks from becoming overwhelming.
- **Variety:** Mix and match ingredients to create a variety of snack jars that cater to different tastes and preferences.

Nutritional Benefits

Snack jars offer a balanced mix of nutrients, combining proteins, healthy fats, and fiber with fresh produce. They are a great way to enjoy wholesome snacks that keep you satisfied and energized throughout the day.

Conclusion

Snack jars provide a convenient and tasty solution for keeping healthy snacks on hand. By preparing these jars in advance, you can enjoy a variety of delicious options that cater to different cravings and dietary needs. With the flexibility to customize and the ease of portability, snack jars are perfect for busy lifestyles and on-the-go snacking.

Healthy Dips and Veggies 4.2.

Introduction

Healthy dips and veggies are the ultimate combination for nutritious snacking. Whether you're looking for a quick and satisfying snack or a wholesome addition to your meal prep, jars filled with vibrant vegetables and flavorful dips offer both convenience and health benefits. This chapter focuses on a selection of dips that are easy to prepare, along with a variety of fresh vegetables to pair them with. These recipes are perfect for meal prep, parties, or a nutritious snack on the go.

Basic Healthy Dip and Veggie Jar Preparation

Ingredients:

- Fresh vegetables (carrots, bell peppers, cucumbers, cherry tomatoes, etc.)
- Healthy dips (such as hummus, guacamole, yogurt-based dips, etc.)
- Optional garnishes (herbs, seeds, or spices)

Instructions:

1. **Prepare Ingredients:** Wash, peel, and cut vegetables into appropriate sizes for dipping. Prepare and portion dips as needed.
2. **Layer Dips and Veggies:** Start with dips at the bottom of the jar to prevent them from mixing with the vegetables. Layer vegetables on top to maintain their crispness.
3. **Seal and Store:** Seal the jar tightly and refrigerate. These jars can typically be stored for up to 3 days.

Healthy Dip and Veggie Jar Recipes

1. Classic Hummus and Veggies Jar

Ingredients:

- 1/4 cup hummus
- 1/2 cup sliced cucumbers
- 1/2 cup cherry tomatoes
- 1/4 cup baby carrots
- 1/4 cup sliced bell peppers

Instructions:

1. **Layer Hummus:** Start with hummus at the bottom of the jar.
2. **Add Vegetables:** Layer sliced cucumbers, cherry tomatoes, baby carrots, and sliced bell peppers on top of the hummus.
3. **Store:** Refrigerate for up to 3 days. Enjoy by dipping the vegetables into the hummus.

2. Creamy Avocado and Veggies Jar

Ingredients:

- 1/4 cup guacamole
- 1/2 cup sliced bell peppers
- 1/2 cup sliced cucumbers
- 1/4 cup cherry tomatoes
- 1/4 cup sliced radishes

Instructions:

1. **Layer Guacamole:** Start with guacamole at the bottom of the jar.
2. **Add Vegetables:** Layer sliced bell peppers, cucumbers, cherry tomatoes, and radishes over the guacamole.
3. **Store:** Refrigerate for up to 3 days. Enjoy with a spoon or use the vegetables to scoop up the guacamole.

3. Greek Yogurt Ranch Dip and Veggies Jar

Ingredients:

- 1/4 cup Greek yogurt ranch dip
- 1/2 cup baby carrots
- 1/2 cup sliced celery
- 1/4 cup cherry tomatoes
- 1/4 cup sliced bell peppers

Instructions:

1. **Layer Dip:** Start with Greek yogurt ranch dip at the bottom of the jar.
2. **Add Vegetables:** Layer baby carrots, sliced celery, cherry tomatoes, and sliced bell peppers over the dip.
3. **Store:** Refrigerate for up to 3 days. Use the vegetables to dip into the Greek yogurt ranch dip.

4. Spicy Red Pepper Dip and Veggies Jar

Ingredients:

- 1/4 cup roasted red pepper dip
- 1/2 cup sliced cucumbers
- 1/2 cup sliced bell peppers
- 1/4 cup cherry tomatoes
- 1/4 cup sugar snap peas

Instructions:

1. **Layer Dip:** Start with roasted red pepper dip at the bottom of the jar.
2. **Add Vegetables:** Layer sliced cucumbers, sliced bell peppers, cherry tomatoes, and sugar snap peas on top of the dip.
3. **Store:** Refrigerate for up to 3 days. Enjoy with a spoon or dip the vegetables into the red pepper dip.

5. Herbed Yogurt Dip and Veggies Jar

Ingredients:

- 1/4 cup herbed yogurt dip (mixed with fresh herbs like dill, chives, and parsley)
- 1/2 cup sliced radishes
- 1/2 cup sliced cucumbers
- 1/4 cup cherry tomatoes
- 1/4 cup baby bell peppers

Instructions:

1. **Layer Dip:** Start with herbed yogurt dip at the bottom of the jar.
2. **Add Vegetables:** Layer sliced radishes, cucumbers, cherry tomatoes, and baby bell peppers over the dip.
3. **Store:** Refrigerate for up to 3 days. Use the vegetables to dip into the herbed yogurt dip.

Tips for Perfect Healthy Dip and Veggie Jars

- **Ingredient Preparation:** Ensure vegetables are cut into appropriate sizes for easy dipping and freshness.
- **Layering:** Place dips at the bottom of the jar to prevent them from mixing with the vegetables and becoming soggy.
- **Portion Control:** Use jars of the right size for your portions to keep snacks manageable and fresh.
- **Garnishing:** Add fresh herbs or a sprinkle of seeds to enhance flavor and presentation.

Nutritional Benefits

Healthy dip and veggie jars are packed with nutrients, including vitamins, minerals, fiber, and healthy fats. They provide a balanced combination of fresh produce and nutrient-rich dips, making them a great choice for a quick, nutritious snack.

Conclusion

Healthy dips and veggies in jars offer a convenient and tasty way to enjoy nutritious snacks throughout the week. With a variety of dips and fresh vegetables to choose from, you can easily customize these jars to suit your tastes and dietary needs. Whether for a quick snack, a meal accompaniment, or a party appetizer, these jars are a practical and delicious solution for maintaining a healthy lifestyle.

Fruit and Nut Mixes 4.3.

Introduction

Fruit and nut mixes are a delicious and versatile option for snacking or meal prep. Combining the natural sweetness of dried fruits with the crunch and protein of nuts creates a satisfying and balanced snack. This chapter showcases a variety of fruit and nut mix recipes that cater to different tastes and dietary preferences. Whether you're looking for a quick energy boost, a nutritious addition to your lunch, or a homemade gift idea, these mixes offer both convenience and flavor.

Basic Fruit and Nut Mix Preparation

Ingredients:

- Dried fruits (such as raisins, cranberries, apricots, or dates)
- Nuts (like almonds, walnuts, cashews, or pecans)
- Optional add-ins (seeds, chocolate chips, coconut flakes, or spices)

Instructions:

1. **Prepare Ingredients:** Chop larger pieces of dried fruit or nuts if necessary. Measure out ingredients for even mixing.
2. **Combine Ingredients:** Mix dried fruits and nuts in a bowl, adjusting proportions to suit your taste.
3. **Add Optional Ingredients:** Incorporate any additional items like seeds, chocolate chips, or spices.
4. **Store:** Transfer the mix to jars or airtight containers. Store at room temperature for up to 2 weeks or refrigerate for extended freshness.

Fruit and Nut Mix Recipes

1. Tropical Delight Mix

Ingredients:

- 1/2 cup dried pineapple chunks
- 1/2 cup dried mango slices
- 1/4 cup coconut flakes
- 1/4 cup cashews
- 1 tablespoon chia seeds

Instructions:

1. **Combine Ingredients:** Mix dried pineapple, dried mango, coconut flakes, and cashews in a bowl.
2. **Add Seeds:** Stir in chia seeds.
3. **Store:** Transfer to jars or airtight containers. Store at room temperature for up to 2 weeks.

2. Berry Nut Crunch Mix

Ingredients:

- 1/2 cup dried blueberries
- 1/2 cup dried raspberries
- 1/4 cup almonds
- 1/4 cup walnuts
- 2 tablespoons dark chocolate chips

Instructions:

1. **Combine Ingredients:** Mix dried blueberries, dried raspberries, almonds, and walnuts i a bowl.
2. **Add Chocolate Chips:** Stir in dark chocolate chips.
3. **Store:** Transfer to jars or airtight containers. Store at room temperature for up to 2 weeks.

3. Classic Trail Mix

Ingredients:

- 1/2 cup raisins
- 1/2 cup dried cranberries
- 1/4 cup sunflower seeds
- 1/4 cup peanuts
- 1/4 cup pretzel sticks

Instructions:

1. **Combine Ingredients:** Mix raisins, dried cranberries, sunflower seeds, peanuts, and pretzel sticks in a bowl.
2. **Store:** Transfer to jars or airtight containers. Store at room temperature for up to 2 weeks.

4. Nutty Apple Cinnamon Mix

Ingredients:

- 1/2 cup dried apple rings
- 1/2 cup almonds
- 1/4 cup pecans
- 1/4 cup pumpkin seeds
- 1/2 teaspoon ground cinnamon

Instructions:

1. **Combine Ingredients:** Mix dried apple rings, almonds, pecans, and pumpkin seeds in bowl.
2. **Add Cinnamon:** Sprinkle ground cinnamon over the mixture and stir well.
3. **Store:** Transfer to jars or airtight containers. Store at room temperature for up to 2 weeks.

5. Spiced Date and Nut Mix

Ingredients:

- 1/2 cup chopped dates
- 1/2 cup walnuts
- 1/4 cup hazelnuts
- 1/4 cup dried figs
- 1/2 teaspoon ground nutmeg

Instructions:

1. **Combine Ingredients:** Mix chopped dates, walnuts, hazelnuts, and dried figs in a bowl.
2. **Add Nutmeg:** Sprinkle ground nutmeg over the mixture and stir well.
3. **Store:** Transfer to jars or airtight containers. Store at room temperature for up to 2 weeks.

Tips for Perfect Fruit and Nut Mixes

- **Ingredient Quality:** Use fresh, high-quality dried fruits and nuts for the best flavor and texture.
- **Mixing Proportions:** Adjust the proportions of fruits and nuts based on personal preference and dietary needs.
- **Add-Ins:** Customize your mix with additional items like seeds, chocolate chips, or spices to enhance flavor and nutrition.
- **Storage:** Keep your mixes in airtight containers to maintain freshness and prevent moisture from affecting the ingredients.

Nutritional Benefits

Fruit and nut mixes provide a great balance of essential nutrients, including healthy fats, protein, fiber, and vitamins. They are an excellent source of sustained energy and can help curb hunger between meals. By incorporating a variety of nuts and fruits, you can enjoy a range of health benefits while satisfying your taste buds.

Conclusion

Fruit and nut mixes are a versatile and delicious snack option that can be tailored to your preferences and dietary requirements. With a variety of recipes and customization options, these mixes offer a convenient way to enjoy wholesome snacks that are both nutritious and satisfying. Whether for a quick energy boost, a nutritious lunch addition, or a homemade gift, these mixes are sure to please.

Protein Snacks 4.4.

Introduction

Protein snacks are essential for maintaining energy levels, supporting muscle growth, and keeping hunger at bay. They are particularly useful for anyone with an active lifestyle or those looking to balance their diet with nutritious, filling options. This chapter focuses on protein-packed snacks that are easy to prepare, store, and enjoy. From savory options to sweet treats, these recipes will help you incorporate more protein into your diet in a convenient and delicious way.

Basic Protein Snack Jar Preparation

Ingredients:

- High-protein foods (such as Greek yogurt, cottage cheese, cooked chicken, tofu, or hard boiled eggs)
- Complementary ingredients (like fresh vegetables, fruits, nuts, or seeds)
- Seasonings and sauces (like herbs, spices, or low-fat dressings)

Instructions:

1. **Prepare Ingredients:** Cook or portion high-protein foods and complementary ingredients. Season or dress as needed.
2. **Layer Ingredients:** Start with protein-rich items at the bottom of the jar. Add complementary ingredients and any seasonings or sauces on top.
3. **Seal and Store:** Seal the jar tightly and refrigerate. Protein snack jars can typically be stored for up to 3 days.

Protein Snack Jar Recipes

1. Greek Yogurt and Berry Bowl

Ingredients:

- 1/2 cup Greek yogurt (plain or vanilla)
- 1/4 cup fresh blueberries
- 1/4 cup fresh strawberries, sliced
- 2 tablespoons chia seeds
- 1 tablespoon honey (optional)

Instructions:

1. **Layer Yogurt:** Start with Greek yogurt at the bottom of the jar.
2. **Add Berries:** Layer fresh blueberries and strawberries on top of the yogurt.
3. **Add Seeds and Sweetener:** Sprinkle chia seeds over the berries and drizzle with honey if desired.
4. **Store:** Refrigerate for up to 3 days. Stir before eating if desired.

2. Chicken Salad with Crackers

Ingredients:

- 1/2 cup cooked, shredded chicken breast
- 1/4 cup Greek yogurt (as a mayo substitute)
- 1 tablespoon Dijon mustard
- 1/4 cup diced celery
- 1/4 cup diced apple
- 1/4 cup whole grain crackers

Instructions:

1. **Prepare Chicken Salad:** In a bowl, mix shredded chicken, Greek yogurt, Dijon mustard, diced celery, and diced apple.
2. **Layer Salad:** Place the chicken salad in the bottom of the jar.
3. **Add Crackers:** Pack whole grain crackers in a separate container or on top of the chicken salad in the jar.
4. **Store:** Refrigerate for up to 3 days. Keep crackers separate until ready to eat to maintain their crunch.

3. Tofu and Veggie Snack Jar

Ingredients:

- 1/2 cup cubed cooked tofu (seasoned or plain)
- 1/2 cup sliced bell peppers
- 1/2 cup cherry tomatoes
- 1/4 cup sliced cucumbers
- 2 tablespoons hummus

Instructions:

1. **Layer Hummus:** Start with hummus at the bottom of the jar.
2. **Add Tofu:** Layer cubed tofu over the hummus.
3. **Add Vegetables:** Layer sliced bell peppers, cherry tomatoes, and cucumbers on top of the tofu.
4. **Store:** Refrigerate for up to 3 days. Enjoy the tofu and veggies with the hummus as a dip.

4. Cottage Cheese and Fruit Parfait

Ingredients:

- 1/2 cup low-fat cottage cheese
- 1/4 cup fresh pineapple chunks
- 1/4 cup diced mango
- 2 tablespoons sunflower seeds
- 1 tablespoon shredded coconut (optional)

Instructions:

1. **Layer Cottage Cheese:** Start with cottage cheese at the bottom of the jar.

2. **Add Fruit:** Layer fresh pineapple chunks and diced mango on top of the cottage cheese.
3. **Add Seeds and Coconut:** Sprinkle sunflower seeds and shredded coconut over the fruit
4. **Store:** Refrigerate for up to 3 days. Stir before eating if desired.

5. Hard-Boiled Eggs and Veggies

Ingredients:

- 2 hard-boiled eggs, peeled
- 1/2 cup sliced cherry tomatoes
- 1/2 cup cucumber slices
- 1/4 cup baby carrots
- 1 tablespoon low-fat ranch dressing

Instructions:

1. **Layer Dressing:** Start with low-fat ranch dressing at the bottom of the jar.
2. **Add Vegetables:** Layer cherry tomatoes, cucumber slices, and baby carrots over the dressing.
3. **Add Eggs:** Place hard-boiled eggs on top of the vegetables.
4. **Store:** Refrigerate for up to 3 days. Enjoy by dipping the vegetables in the ranch dressing and eating the eggs on the side.

Tips for Perfect Protein Snack Jars

- **Ingredient Quality:** Use fresh, high-quality ingredients for the best flavor and nutritional benefits.
- **Layering:** Place protein-rich items at the bottom of the jar to avoid mixing with other ingredients and becoming soggy.
- **Portion Control:** Adjust portion sizes based on your dietary needs and preferences.
- **Storage:** Store jars tightly sealed to maintain freshness and prevent spoilage.

Nutritional Benefits

Protein snacks offer a range of health benefits, including muscle repair, increased satiety, and stable energy levels. By incorporating various protein sources and complementary ingredients, these jars provide a balanced and satisfying option for any time of the day.

Conclusion

Protein snacks in jars are a practical and delicious way to incorporate more protein into your diet. With a variety of recipes and customizable options, these jars offer both convenience and nutrition for busy lifestyles. Whether you need a quick snack or a nutritious meal addition, these protein-packed jars are sure to keep you satisfied and energized.

Quick Energy Boosters

Introduction

When you need a pick-me-up, quick energy boosters are the perfect solution. Whether you're facing an afternoon slump or need a pre-workout snack, these energy-boosting jars are packed with ingredients that provide a rapid and sustained release of energy. Combining protein, healthy fats, and natural sugars, these recipes are designed to keep you alert and satisfied throughout the day. This chapter presents a variety of quick and easy energy-boosting jars that are perfect for busy lifestyles.

Basic Quick Energy Booster Jar Preparation

Ingredients:

- High-energy foods (like nuts, seeds, dried fruits, or whole grains)
- Protein-rich ingredients (such as Greek yogurt, nut butters, or cottage cheese)
- Natural sweeteners (like honey or maple syrup)
- Fresh fruits or vegetables for added vitamins and minerals

Instructions:

1. **Prepare Ingredients:** Chop, measure, and portion ingredients as needed. Ensure all components are fresh and ready for layering.
2. **Layer Ingredients:** Begin with items that may release moisture or become soggy, like yogurt or nut butters, and layer drier ingredients on top.
3. **Seal and Store:** Seal jars tightly and store in the refrigerator if needed. These jars can typically be stored for up to 3 days.

Quick Energy Booster Jar Recipes

1. Nut Butter and Banana Jar

Ingredients:

- 2 tablespoons almond or peanut butter
- 1/2 banana, sliced
- 1/4 cup granola
- 1 tablespoon chia seeds

Instructions:

1. **Layer Nut Butter:** Start with almond or peanut butter at the bottom of the jar.
2. **Add Banana:** Layer banana slices on top of the nut butter.
3. **Add Granola and Seeds:** Sprinkle granola and chia seeds over the banana slices.
4. **Store:** Refrigerate for up to 2 days. Stir before eating if desired.

2. Berry and Oat Energy Jar

Ingredients:

- 1/2 cup Greek yogurt (plain or vanilla)
- 1/4 cup rolled oats
- 1/4 cup mixed berries (blueberries, raspberries, strawberries)
- 1 tablespoon honey or maple syrup

Instructions:

1. **Layer Yogurt:** Start with Greek yogurt at the bottom of the jar.
2. **Add Oats:** Layer rolled oats over the yogurt.
3. **Add Berries:** Place mixed berries on top of the oats.
4. **Drizzle with Sweetener:** Drizzle honey or maple syrup over the top.
5. **Store:** Refrigerate for up to 2 days. Stir before eating if desired.

3. Cottage Cheese and Fruit Energy Jar

Ingredients:

- 1/2 cup low-fat cottage cheese
- 1/4 cup diced pineapple
- 1/4 cup diced mango
- 2 tablespoons sunflower seeds
- 1 tablespoon shredded coconut (optional)

Instructions:

1. **Layer Cottage Cheese:** Start with cottage cheese at the bottom of the jar.
2. **Add Fruit:** Layer diced pineapple and mango over the cottage cheese.
3. **Add Seeds and Coconut:** Sprinkle sunflower seeds and shredded coconut over the frui
4. **Store:** Refrigerate for up to 2 days. Stir before eating if desired.

4. Quick Protein-Packed Smoothie Jar

Ingredients:

- 1/2 cup Greek yogurt
- 1/2 cup frozen mixed berries
- 1 tablespoon protein powder
- 1 tablespoon flaxseeds

Instructions:

1. **Layer Yogurt:** Start with Greek yogurt at the bottom of the jar.
2. **Add Berries and Protein Powder:** Layer frozen mixed berries and protein powder on top of the yogurt.
3. **Add Flaxseeds:** Sprinkle flaxseeds over the top.
4. **Store:** Refrigerate for up to 2 days. Blend before consuming if desired.

5. Energy Nut and Fruit Mix Jar

Ingredients:

- 1/4 cup almonds
- 1/4 cup walnuts
- 1/4 cup dried cranberries
- 1/4 cup dried apricots, chopped
- 1 tablespoon pumpkin seeds

Instructions:

1. **Combine Ingredients:** Mix almonds, walnuts, dried cranberries, dried apricots, and pumpkin seeds in a bowl.
2. **Store:** Transfer to jars or airtight containers. Store at room temperature for up to 1 week.

Tips for Perfect Quick Energy Boosters

- **Ingredient Quality:** Use fresh, high-quality ingredients to maximize flavor and nutritional benefits.
- **Portion Control:** Adjust portion sizes based on your energy needs and dietary preferences.
- **Mix and Match:** Experiment with different combinations of fruits, nuts, seeds, and protein sources to find your favorite energy-boosting mix.
- **Storage:** Keep jars tightly sealed and refrigerated if necessary to maintain freshness.

Nutritional Benefits

Quick energy boosters are designed to provide a balanced mix of protein, healthy fats, and carbohydrates. These components work together to offer sustained energy, support muscle function, and prevent hunger. By incorporating a variety of nutrient-dense ingredients, these jars help maintain stable energy levels throughout the day.

Conclusion

Quick energy boosters in jars are a practical and delicious way to keep your energy levels up and your cravings in check. With a variety of recipes and customization options, these jars provide a convenient solution for busy lifestyles and active individuals. Whether you need a quick snack or a pre-workout boost, these energy-boosting jars are sure to help you power through your day.

Chapter 5:

Dessert Jars 5.1.

Introduction

Dessert jars are a delightful way to enjoy sweet treats with minimal fuss. Perfect for portion control, meal prep, or a quick indulgence, these jarred desserts offer a mix of convenience and creativity. Whether you're craving a classic pudding, a decadent cheesecake, or a fruity parfait, dessert jars provide an easy solution for satisfying your sweet tooth. This chapter explores a variety of dessert jar recipes that are not only delicious but also easy to prepare and perfect for any occasion.

Basic Dessert Jar Preparation

Ingredients:

- Base ingredients (such as yogurt, pudding, or cheesecake filling)
- Layering components (like fruit, granola, or chocolate)
- Sweeteners and flavorings (such as honey, vanilla extract, or cocoa powder)

Instructions:

1. **Prepare Ingredients:** Cook, bake, or mix base ingredients as needed. Prepare and chop additional components for layering.
2. **Layer Ingredients:** Start with base ingredients at the bottom of the jar, followed by layering components. Repeat layers as desired.
3. **Chill or Serve:** Some dessert jars benefit from chilling in the refrigerator to enhance flavors and texture. Others can be enjoyed immediately.

Dessert Jar Recipes

1. Classic Chocolate Pudding Jar

Ingredients:

- 1/2 cup chocolate pudding (store-bought or homemade)
- 1/4 cup crushed graham crackers
- 2 tablespoons mini marshmallows
- 1 tablespoon chocolate chips

Instructions:

1. **Layer Pudding:** Start with chocolate pudding at the bottom of the jar.
2. **Add Graham Crackers:** Layer crushed graham crackers over the pudding.
3. **Add Marshmallows and Chocolate Chips:** Top with mini marshmallows and chocolate chips.
4. **Chill:** Refrigerate for at least 30 minutes before serving to let the flavors meld.

2. Berry Yogurt Parfait

Ingredients:

- 1/2 cup Greek yogurt (plain or vanilla)
- 1/4 cup fresh mixed berries (strawberries, blueberries, raspberries)
- 2 tablespoons granola
- 1 tablespoon honey

Instructions:

1. **Layer Yogurt:** Start with Greek yogurt at the bottom of the jar.
2. **Add Berries:** Layer fresh mixed berries on top of the yogurt.
3. **Add Granola and Honey:** Sprinkle granola and drizzle with honey.
4. **Serve:** Enjoy immediately or refrigerate for up to 2 days.

3. No-Bake Cheesecake Jar

Ingredients:

- 1/2 cup cheesecake filling (store-bought or homemade)
- 1/4 cup crushed graham crackers
- 1/4 cup fresh strawberries, sliced
- 1 tablespoon strawberry sauce or jam

Instructions:

1. **Layer Cheesecake Filling:** Start with cheesecake filling at the bottom of the jar.
2. **Add Graham Crackers:** Layer crushed graham crackers over the cheesecake.
3. **Add Strawberries and Sauce:** Top with fresh strawberries and a drizzle of strawberry sauce or jam.
4. **Chill:** Refrigerate for at least 1 hour before serving.

4. Apple Cinnamon Oat Dessert Jar

Ingredients:

- 1/2 cup cooked oatmeal (cooled)
- 1/4 cup diced apples
- 1 tablespoon cinnamon
- 1 tablespoon maple syrup

Instructions:

1. **Layer Oatmeal:** Start with cooked oatmeal at the bottom of the jar.
2. **Add Apples and Cinnamon:** Layer diced apples and sprinkle with cinnamon.
3. **Drizzle with Maple Syrup:** Top with a drizzle of maple syrup.
4. **Serve:** Enjoy immediately or refrigerate for up to 2 days.

5. Peach Cobbler in a Jar

Ingredients:

- 1/2 cup canned or fresh peach slices
- 1/4 cup crumbled vanilla cake or muffin
- 1 tablespoon brown sugar
- 1/4 teaspoon ground cinnamon

Instructions:

1. **Layer Peaches:** Start with peach slices at the bottom of the jar.
2. **Add Cake Crumbs:** Layer crumbled vanilla cake or muffin over the peaches.
3. **Sprinkle with Sugar and Cinnamon:** Top with brown sugar and ground cinnamon.
4. **Serve:** Enjoy immediately or warm slightly before serving.

Tips for Perfect Dessert Jars

- **Ingredient Quality:** Use fresh or high-quality ingredients for the best flavor and texture
- **Layering:** For a visually appealing jar, layer ingredients carefully and creatively.
- **Sweeteners:** Adjust sweeteners according to your taste preference and dietary needs.
- **Chilling:** Many dessert jars benefit from chilling to enhance flavor and texture.

Nutritional Benefits

While dessert jars are indulgent, they can be made with healthier ingredients to fit into a balanced diet. By using Greek yogurt, fresh fruit, and reducing added sugars, you can enjoy a sweet treat that is also nutritious. These jars offer a way to enjoy dessert while still maintaining focus on health.

Conclusion

Dessert jars are a fun and convenient way to enjoy your favorite sweet treats. With a variety of recipes to suit different tastes and dietary preferences, these jars are perfect for satisfying your cravings without compromising on convenience. Whether you're preparing for a party, a quick dessert, or a meal prep, these jarred desserts offer delicious solutions for your sweet tooth.

Fruit-Based Desserts 5.2.

Introduction

Fruit-based desserts are a delightful and refreshing way to enjoy nature's sweets. Packed with vitamins, fiber, and natural sugars, these desserts are not only delicious but also offer a healthie alternative to traditional sweets. Whether you're looking for a quick treat or a sophisticated dessert for a special occasion, fruit-based desserts in jars are perfect for any situation. This chapter explores a variety of fruity delights that are easy to prepare and enjoy, combining vibra flavors and appealing textures.

Basic Fruit-Based Dessert Jar Preparation

Ingredients:

- Fresh or frozen fruits
- Base ingredients (like yogurt, pudding, or a crumbly topping)
- Sweeteners (such as honey, agave, or maple syrup)
- Optional add-ins (like nuts, seeds, or granola)

Instructions:

1. **Prepare Ingredients:** Wash, chop, and prepare fruits. Prepare base ingredients and optional add-ins.
2. **Layer Ingredients:** Start with base ingredients at the bottom of the jar, followed by fruit layers and any additional toppings.
3. **Chill or Serve:** Some desserts benefit from chilling to enhance flavors, while others can be enjoyed immediately.

Fruit-Based Dessert Jar Recipes

1. Mango Coconut Chia Pudding

Ingredients:

- 1/2 cup chia seeds
- 1 cup coconut milk
- 1 tablespoon honey or maple syrup
- 1/2 cup fresh mango, diced
- 2 tablespoons shredded coconut

Instructions:

1. **Prepare Chia Pudding:** In a bowl, mix chia seeds, coconut milk, and honey or maple syrup. Let sit for at least 30 minutes or overnight in the refrigerator until thickened.
2. **Layer Pudding:** Spoon chia pudding into the bottom of the jar.
3. **Add Mango and Coconut:** Top with fresh mango and shredded coconut.
4. **Chill:** Refrigerate for at least 1 hour before serving.

2. Berry Yogurt Crumble

Ingredients:

- 1/2 cup Greek yogurt (plain or vanilla)
- 1/2 cup mixed berries (blueberries, raspberries, strawberries)
- 1/4 cup granola
- 1 tablespoon honey

Instructions:

1. **Layer Yogurt:** Start with Greek yogurt at the bottom of the jar.
2. **Add Berries:** Layer mixed berries over the yogurt.
3. **Add Granola:** Sprinkle granola on top of the berries.

4. **Drizzle with Honey:** Drizzle honey over the granola.
5. **Serve:** Enjoy immediately or refrigerate for up to 2 days.

3. Apple Cinnamon Delight

Ingredients:

- 1/2 cup unsweetened applesauce
- 1/4 cup diced apples
- 1/4 teaspoon ground cinnamon
- 2 tablespoons crushed graham crackers

Instructions:

1. **Layer Applesauce:** Start with applesauce at the bottom of the jar.
2. **Add Diced Apples:** Layer diced apples on top of the applesauce.
3. **Sprinkle Cinnamon:** Sprinkle ground cinnamon over the apples.
4. **Add Graham Crackers:** Top with crushed graham crackers.
5. **Serve:** Enjoy immediately or refrigerate for up to 2 days.

4. Peach Yogurt Parfait

Ingredients:

- 1/2 cup vanilla yogurt
- 1/4 cup canned or fresh peach slices
- 1/4 cup granola
- 1 tablespoon almond slices

Instructions:

1. **Layer Yogurt:** Start with vanilla yogurt at the bottom of the jar.
2. **Add Peach Slices:** Layer peach slices on top of the yogurt.
3. **Add Granola and Almonds:** Sprinkle granola and almond slices over the peaches.
4. **Serve:** Enjoy immediately or refrigerate for up to 2 days.

5. Berry and Banana Oat Crumble

Ingredients:

- 1/2 cup cooked oats
- 1/4 cup fresh strawberries, sliced
- 1/4 cup fresh blueberries
- 1/2 banana, sliced
- 2 tablespoons almond butter
- 1 tablespoon honey

Instructions:

1. **Layer Oats:** Start with cooked oats at the bottom of the jar.
2. **Add Fruits:** Layer strawberries, blueberries, and banana slices on top of the oats.
3. **Add Almond Butter and Honey:** Drizzle almond butter and honey over the fruit.

4. **Serve:** Enjoy immediately or refrigerate for up to 2 days.

Tips for Perfect Fruit-Based Desserts

- **Ingredient Quality:** Use fresh, ripe fruits for the best flavor and texture.
- **Layering:** Create visually appealing layers by varying colors and textures.
- **Sweeteners:** Adjust sweeteners according to the natural sweetness of the fruits and personal preference.
- **Chilling:** Some desserts benefit from chilling to enhance flavor and texture.

Nutritional Benefits

Fruit-based desserts offer a range of health benefits, including high levels of vitamins, minerals, and fiber. They are a great way to satisfy a sweet craving while still maintaining a focus on health. Incorporating fruits into your desserts helps boost your daily fruit intake and provides a natural source of energy and antioxidants.

Conclusion

Fruit-based desserts in jars are a delicious and convenient way to enjoy the natural sweetness of fruits. With a variety of recipes to suit different tastes and dietary needs, these jars offer a perfect solution for a quick, healthy, and satisfying treat. Whether you're preparing for a special occasion or simply looking for a refreshing snack, these fruit-based desserts are sure to delight.

No-Bake Treats 5.4.

Introduction

No-bake treats are the epitome of convenience and deliciousness. They are perfect for when you crave a sweet indulgence without the time or effort required for baking. These treats are quick to prepare, require minimal equipment, and often involve simple, wholesome ingredients. Whether you're looking for a nutritious snack, a decadent dessert, or something in between, no-bake treats in jars offer a range of options to suit every taste. This chapter presents a variety of no-bake recipes that are easy to assemble and perfect for satisfying your sweet tooth.

Basic No-Bake Treat Jar Preparation

Ingredients:

- Base ingredients (such as oats, nuts, or coconut)

- Binding agents (like nut butters, honey, or maple syrup)
- Flavorings and add-ins (such as chocolate chips, dried fruits, or spices)

Instructions:

1. **Prepare Ingredients:** Measure and mix base ingredients and binding agents. Chop any add-ins as needed.
2. **Combine Ingredients:** Mix ingredients thoroughly until well combined.
3. **Layer or Pack:** Depending on the recipe, either layer the mixture in jars or press it down firmly.
4. **Chill or Set:** Refrigerate or freeze as required to set the treats before serving.

No-Bake Treat Jar Recipes

1. Chocolate Peanut Butter Energy Balls

Ingredients:

- 1 cup oats
- 1/2 cup peanut butter
- 1/4 cup honey
- 1/4 cup cocoa powder
- 1/4 cup mini chocolate chips

Instructions:

1. **Mix Ingredients:** In a bowl, combine oats, peanut butter, honey, and cocoa powder until well mixed.
2. **Add Chocolate Chips:** Stir in mini chocolate chips.
3. **Form Balls:** Roll the mixture into small balls and place in jars.
4. **Chill:** Refrigerate for at least 30 minutes before serving.

2. Coconut Almond Energy Bars

Ingredients:

- 1 cup almonds, chopped
- 1 cup shredded coconut
- 1/2 cup almond butter
- 1/4 cup honey
- 1/4 cup dried cranberries

Instructions:

1. **Mix Ingredients:** In a bowl, combine chopped almonds, shredded coconut, almond butter, and honey.
2. **Add Cranberries:** Stir in dried cranberries.
3. **Press into Jars:** Press the mixture firmly into the bottom of jars or a lined baking dish.
4. **Chill:** Refrigerate for at least 1 hour to set before cutting into bars.

3. Berry Chia Seed Pudding

Ingredients:

- 1/4 cup chia seeds
- 1 cup almond milk
- 1 tablespoon honey or maple syrup
- 1/2 cup fresh mixed berries (strawberries, blueberries, raspberries)

Instructions:

1. **Prepare Chia Pudding:** In a bowl, mix chia seeds, almond milk, and honey or maple syrup. Let sit for at least 30 minutes or overnight in the refrigerator.
2. **Layer Pudding:** Spoon chia pudding into the bottom of the jar.
3. **Add Berries:** Top with fresh mixed berries.
4. **Chill:** Refrigerate for at least 1 hour before serving.

4. No-Bake Cheesecake Jars

Ingredients:

- 1/2 cup graham cracker crumbs
- 1/4 cup melted butter
- 1 cup cream cheese
- 1/2 cup Greek yogurt
- 1/4 cup honey
- 1/2 teaspoon vanilla extract
- Fresh fruit or fruit sauce for topping

Instructions:

1. **Prepare Crust:** Mix graham cracker crumbs and melted butter. Press into the bottom of the jars.
2. **Prepare Cheesecake Filling:** In a bowl, combine cream cheese, Greek yogurt, honey, and vanilla extract. Mix until smooth.
3. **Layer Filling:** Spoon cheesecake filling over the crust in the jars.
4. **Add Topping:** Top with fresh fruit or fruit sauce.
5. **Chill:** Refrigerate for at least 2 hours before serving.

5. Nut and Date Energy Bars

Ingredients:

- 1 cup pitted dates
- 1 cup mixed nuts (almonds, walnuts, cashews)
- 1/4 cup flaxseeds
- 1 tablespoon coconut oil
- 1 tablespoon cocoa powder

Instructions:

1. **Blend Ingredients:** In a food processor, blend dates, mixed nuts, flaxseeds, coconut oil, and cocoa powder until finely chopped and well combined.

2. **Press into Jars:** Press the mixture firmly into the bottom of jars or a lined baking dish.
3. **Chill:** Refrigerate for at least 1 hour before cutting into bars.

Tips for Perfect No-Bake Treats

- **Ingredient Quality:** Use fresh, high-quality ingredients for the best flavor and texture.
- **Mixing:** Ensure ingredients are thoroughly mixed for even flavor and consistency.
- **Setting:** Allow adequate time for chilling or freezing to ensure treats are properly set.
- **Portioning:** For easy serving, consider portioning treats into individual jars or containers.

Nutritional Benefits

No-bake treats often feature wholesome ingredients like nuts, seeds, and fruits, providing a good source of protein, fiber, and healthy fats. They offer a healthier alternative to traditional sweets and can be customized to fit various dietary preferences. By incorporating nutrient-dense ingredients, these treats support overall health while satisfying your sweet cravings.

Conclusion

No-bake treats in jars are a fantastic way to enjoy sweet indulgences with minimal effort and maximum flavor. With a variety of recipes to suit different tastes and dietary needs, these treats are perfect for quick snacks, meal prep, or special occasions. Enjoy the convenience and deliciousness of no-bake desserts that make satisfying your sweet tooth easier than ever.

Mini Cakes and Pies

Introduction

Mini cakes and pies are the perfect solution for those who crave a sweet treat but want to enjoy it in a more controlled portion. These delightful jarred desserts offer the rich flavors and comforting textures of classic cakes and pies without the need for a full-sized baking endeavor. Ideal for parties, personal indulgence, or meal prepping, mini cakes and pies in jars combine the convenience of portion control with the indulgence of homemade desserts. This chapter explore various recipes for mini cakes and pies that are easy to prepare, serve, and enjoy.

Basic Mini Cake and Pie Jar Preparation

Ingredients:

- Base ingredients (such as cake or pie crust components)
- Filling ingredients (like fruits, custards, or cream)
- Topping ingredients (such as frosting, whipped cream, or crumb toppings)

Instructions:

1. **Prepare Ingredients:** Mix or cook base ingredients and prepare filling components.
2. **Layer Ingredients:** Begin with the base layer at the bottom of the jar, followed by fillings and toppings.
3. **Chill or Bake:** Some recipes require baking, while others benefit from chilling to set flavors and textures.

Mini Cake and Pie Jar Recipes

1. Mini Chocolate Lava Cakes

Ingredients:

- 1/2 cup unsalted butter
- 1/2 cup semi-sweet chocolate chips
- 1 cup powdered sugar
- 2 large eggs
- 2 large egg yolks
- 1/2 cup all-purpose flour
- Butter and cocoa powder for greasing jars

Instructions:

1. **Prepare Jars:** Grease the inside of small mason jars with butter and dust with cocoa powder.
2. **Melt Butter and Chocolate:** In a microwave-safe bowl, melt butter and chocolate chips together until smooth.
3. **Mix Batter:** Stir in powdered sugar, eggs, and egg yolks. Mix well. Add flour and mix until just combined.
4. **Fill Jars:** Spoon batter into prepared jars, filling them about 2/3 full.
5. **Bake:** Place jars on a baking sheet and bake at 425°F (220°C) for 12-15 minutes, or until the edges are set but the center remains soft.
6. **Serve:** Allow to cool slightly before serving. Top with a scoop of vanilla ice cream if desired.

2. Mini Apple Pies

Ingredients:

- 1 pie dough (store-bought or homemade)
- 2 cups apples, peeled and diced
- 1/4 cup brown sugar
- 1 tablespoon all-purpose flour
- 1/2 teaspoon cinnamon
- 1/4 teaspoon nutmeg
- 1 tablespoon unsalted butter, diced

Instructions:

1. **Prepare Jars:** Cut pie dough into circles slightly larger than the diameter of the jars and press into the bottom and up the sides of each jar.
2. **Mix Filling:** In a bowl, combine diced apples, brown sugar, flour, cinnamon, and nutmeg.
3. **Fill Jars:** Spoon the apple mixture into the prepared pie crusts. Dot with small pieces of butter.
4. **Top with Dough:** Cut additional pie dough into strips or shapes and place on top of the apple filling.
5. **Bake:** Place jars on a baking sheet and bake at 375°F (190°C) for 30-35 minutes, or until the crust is golden brown and the filling is bubbly.
6. **Serve:** Let cool slightly before serving.

3. Mini Lemon Cheesecakes

Ingredients:

- 1/2 cup graham cracker crumbs
- 2 tablespoons unsalted butter, melted
- 8 oz cream cheese, softened
- 1/2 cup granulated sugar
- 1/2 cup sour cream
- 2 large eggs
- Zest and juice of 1 lemon
- Fresh berries for garnish

Instructions:

1. **Prepare Crust:** Mix graham cracker crumbs and melted butter. Press into the bottom of each jar.
2. **Prepare Filling:** In a bowl, beat cream cheese until smooth. Add sugar, sour cream, eggs, lemon zest, and lemon juice. Mix until well combined.
3. **Fill Jars:** Spoon cheesecake filling over the crust in each jar.
4. **Bake:** Place jars in a baking dish filled with water (to create a water bath) and bake at 325°F (163°C) for 25-30 minutes, or until the center is set.
5. **Chill:** Let cool completely, then refrigerate for at least 2 hours before serving.
6. **Garnish:** Top with fresh berries before serving.

4. Mini Carrot Cake Jars

Ingredients:

- 1 cup all-purpose flour
- 1/2 cup granulated sugar
- 1/2 teaspoon baking powder
- 1/2 teaspoon baking soda
- 1/2 teaspoon ground cinnamon
- 1/4 teaspoon ground nutmeg
- 1/4 teaspoon salt
- 1/2 cup grated carrots
- 1/4 cup crushed pineapple, drained
- 1/4 cup chopped walnuts

- 1/4 cup vegetable oil
- 1 large egg
- Cream cheese frosting for topping

Instructions:

1. **Prepare Batter:** In a bowl, mix flour, sugar, baking powder, baking soda, cinnamon, nutmeg, and salt. Stir in grated carrots, crushed pineapple, walnuts, vegetable oil, and egg. Mix until combined.
2. **Fill Jars:** Spoon batter into the bottom of each jar, filling about halfway.
3. **Bake:** Place jars on a baking sheet and bake at 350°F (175°C) for 20-25 minutes, or until a toothpick inserted into the center comes out clean.
4. **Cool and Frost:** Let cakes cool completely before frosting with cream cheese frosting.

5. Mini Key Lime Pies

Ingredients:

- 1 cup graham cracker crumbs
- 1/4 cup granulated sugar
- 1/4 cup unsalted butter, melted
- 1 cup sweetened condensed milk
- 1/2 cup key lime juice
- 2 large egg yolks
- Whipped cream for topping

Instructions:

1. **Prepare Crust:** Mix graham cracker crumbs, sugar, and melted butter. Press into the bottom of each jar.
2. **Prepare Filling:** In a bowl, mix sweetened condensed milk, key lime juice, and egg yolks until smooth.
3. **Fill Jars:** Spoon the lime filling over the crusts in each jar.
4. **Bake:** Place jars on a baking sheet and bake at 325°F (163°C) for 15-20 minutes, or until the filling is set.
5. **Chill:** Let cool completely, then refrigerate for at least 1 hour before serving.
6. **Top with Whipped Cream:** Add a dollop of whipped cream before serving.

Tips for Perfect Mini Cakes and Pies

- **Ingredient Preparation:** Ensure all ingredients are measured accurately and prepared in advance to streamline the process.
- **Portion Control:** Use appropriately sized jars to achieve the desired portion size for each mini cake or pie.
- **Baking Time:** Adjust baking times based on jar size and oven performance. Check for doneness with a toothpick.
- **Chilling:** Many mini desserts benefit from chilling to enhance flavor and texture.

Nutritional Benefits

Mini cakes and pies can be made with healthier ingredients, such as whole grains, reduced sugar, or natural sweeteners, to offer a more balanced treat. By incorporating fruits, nuts, and other wholesome ingredients, these desserts can provide additional nutrients while still indulging your sweet cravings.

Conclusion

Mini cakes and pies in jars offer a charming and convenient way to enjoy your favorite desserts in a perfectly portioned size. With a variety of recipes to suit different tastes and dietary preferences, these jarred treats are ideal for any occasion, whether it's a casual snack or a special celebration. Enjoy the ease and deliciousness of mini desserts that make satisfying your sweet tooth simple and delightful.

Chapter 6:

Kid-Friendly Jars 6.1.

Introduction

Kid-friendly jars are a fantastic way to make mealtime and snack time fun, nutritious, and convenient. Whether you're looking for healthy options for school lunches, easy after-school snacks, or a creative way to get kids excited about eating, these jarred recipes offer something for every young palate. From colorful fruit parfaits to playful mini pizzas, these recipes are designed to be both appealing and practical, encouraging kids to enjoy a variety of foods while simplifying meal prep for busy families. This chapter features a range of jarred recipes that are sure to delight children and make mealtime easier for parents.

Basic Kid-Friendly Jar Preparation

Ingredients:

- Fresh fruits and vegetables
- Protein sources (like yogurt, cheese, or chicken)
- Whole grains (such as oats, whole wheat crackers, or rice)
- Fun add-ins (like sprinkles, mini chocolate chips, or colorful veggies)

Instructions:

1. **Prepare Ingredients:** Wash, chop, and measure ingredients. Prepare any additional components like sauces or dressings.
2. **Layer Ingredients:** Start with base ingredients in the jar, followed by proteins, grains, and any fun add-ins.

3. **Serve or Store:** Depending on the recipe, jars can be served immediately or stored in the refrigerator for later.

Kid-Friendly Jar Recipes

1. Fruit and Yogurt Parfait

Ingredients:

- 1/2 cup vanilla yogurt
- 1/4 cup fresh strawberries, sliced
- 1/4 cup blueberries
- 2 tablespoons granola
- 1 tablespoon honey

Instructions:

1. **Layer Yogurt:** Start with vanilla yogurt at the bottom of the jar.
2. **Add Fruit:** Layer strawberries and blueberries on top of the yogurt.
3. **Add Granola:** Sprinkle granola over the fruit.
4. **Drizzle with Honey:** Add a drizzle of honey for extra sweetness.
5. **Serve:** Enjoy immediately or refrigerate for up to 2 days.

2. Mini Pizza Jars

Ingredients:

- 1/2 cup marinara sauce
- 1/2 cup shredded mozzarella cheese
- 1/4 cup mini pepperoni slices
- 1/4 cup diced bell peppers
- 1/4 cup sliced black olives
- 1/2 cup whole wheat pita bread, cut into small pieces

Instructions:

1. **Layer Ingredients:** Start with a spoonful of marinara sauce at the bottom of the jar.
2. **Add Cheese:** Sprinkle shredded mozzarella cheese over the sauce.
3. **Add Toppings:** Layer mini pepperoni slices, diced bell peppers, and black olives.
4. **Add Pita Bread:** Top with small pieces of pita bread.
5. **Serve:** Enjoy immediately, or heat in the microwave for a warm, melty treat.

3. Rainbow Veggie and Hummus Jars

Ingredients:

- 1/2 cup hummus
- 1/4 cup sliced cherry tomatoes
- 1/4 cup sliced cucumbers
- 1/4 cup shredded carrots

- 1/4 cup bell pepper strips
- 1/4 cup snap peas

Instructions:

1. **Layer Hummus:** Start with hummus at the bottom of the jar.
2. **Add Veggies:** Layer cherry tomatoes, cucumbers, shredded carrots, bell pepper strips, and snap peas on top of the hummus.
3. **Serve:** Enjoy immediately for a crunchy, colorful snack or meal.

4. Nut Butter and Banana Oat Jars

Ingredients:

- 1/2 cup rolled oats
- 1/4 cup almond or peanut butter
- 1/4 cup milk (or non-dairy alternative)
- 1/2 banana, sliced
- 1 tablespoon chia seeds

Instructions:

1. **Mix Oats and Milk:** In a bowl, combine rolled oats and milk. Stir well.
2. **Add Nut Butter:** Mix in almond or peanut butter until smooth.
3. **Layer in Jar:** Spoon oat mixture into the jar, then add banana slices and chia seeds.
4. **Serve:** Enjoy immediately or refrigerate overnight for a quick, nutritious breakfast.

5. DIY Trail Mix Jars

Ingredients:

- 1/4 cup pretzel sticks
- 1/4 cup dried cranberries
- 1/4 cup roasted almonds
- 1/4 cup mini chocolate chips
- 1/4 cup sunflower seeds

Instructions:

1. **Combine Ingredients:** In a bowl, mix pretzel sticks, dried cranberries, roasted almonds, mini chocolate chips, and sunflower seeds.
2. **Fill Jars:** Spoon the trail mix into jars.
3. **Serve:** Perfect as a portable snack or a fun addition to lunchboxes.

Tips for Perfect Kid-Friendly Jars

- **Involvement:** Get kids involved in preparing their own jars to increase their interest in the food they're eating.
- **Variety:** Use a mix of colorful fruits and vegetables to make the jars visually appealing
- **Portion Control:** Use jars with appropriate sizes to help with portion control and prevent overeating.
- **Storage:** Store jars in the refrigerator to keep ingredients fresh and crunchy.

Nutritional Benefits

Kid-friendly jars often include a mix of fruits, vegetables, and protein sources, offering a balanced approach to snacking and meals. Incorporating a variety of colorful ingredients ensures that kids get essential vitamins and minerals. These jars also help in developing healthy eating habits by providing nutritious options in a fun and accessible way.

Conclusion

Kid-friendly jars make mealtime and snack time enjoyable and stress-free for both kids and parents. With a range of recipes that cater to different tastes and preferences, these jars are perfect for encouraging healthy eating habits and simplifying meal preparation. Enjoy the convenience and creativity of jarred meals that make eating fun and nutritious.

School Lunch Ideas 6.3.

Introduction

Packing a school lunch that is both nutritious and appealing can be a challenge for parents. Jars offer a practical and creative solution for preparing and storing school lunches that kids will enjoy. From hearty salads to fun, portable wraps, these jarred recipes are designed to be easy to prepare, nutritious, and appealing to young taste buds. This chapter provides a variety of school lunch ideas that can be assembled in advance, making lunchtime a breeze for busy families.

Basic School Lunch Jar Preparation

Ingredients:

- Fresh vegetables and fruits
- Protein sources (such as chicken, tofu, or cheese)
- Grains and legumes (like quinoa, rice, or beans)
- Dressings and dips (for added flavor and nutrition)
- Fun extras (like crackers, nuts, or dried fruit)

Instructions:

1. **Prepare Ingredients:** Wash, chop, and cook ingredients as needed. Prepare dressings or dips.
2. **Layer Ingredients:** Start with heavier items like grains or proteins at the bottom of the jar, followed by vegetables and fruits. Keep dressings or dips separate until ready to eat.
3. **Seal and Store:** Seal jars tightly and store them in the refrigerator until lunchtime.

School Lunch Jar Recipes

1. Chicken Caesar Salad Jars

Ingredients:

- 1/2 cup cooked chicken breast, diced
- 1 cup chopped romaine lettuce
- 1/4 cup grated Parmesan cheese
- 1/4 cup croutons
- 2 tablespoons Caesar dressing

Instructions:

1. **Layer Ingredients:** Start with Caesar dressing at the bottom of the jar.
2. **Add Chicken:** Layer diced chicken breast on top of the dressing.
3. **Add Cheese and Croutons:** Add grated Parmesan cheese and croutons.
4. **Top with Lettuce:** Finish with chopped romaine lettuce.
5. **Serve:** Shake jar to mix ingredients before eating, or pack the dressing separately.

2. Turkey and Cheese Roll-Up Jars

Ingredients:

- 4 slices turkey breast
- 2 slices cheese (Swiss or cheddar)
- 1/4 cup sliced cucumber
- 1/4 cup cherry tomatoes, halved
- 1 tablespoon hummus

Instructions:

1. **Prepare Roll-Ups:** Spread hummus on turkey slices, then place a slice of cheese on top. Roll up the turkey and cheese together and slice into bite-sized pieces.
2. **Layer Jar:** Place turkey and cheese roll-ups in the jar, followed by cucumber slices and cherry tomatoes.
3. **Serve:** Enjoy immediately or pack with a side of hummus for dipping.

3. Quinoa and Veggie Power Bowl

Ingredients:

- 1/2 cup cooked quinoa
- 1/4 cup diced bell peppers
- 1/4 cup shredded carrots
- 1/4 cup black beans, rinsed
- 1/4 cup corn kernels
- 2 tablespoons avocado dressing

Instructions:

1. **Layer Ingredients:** Start with quinoa at the bottom of the jar.

2. **Add Veggies:** Layer diced bell peppers, shredded carrots, black beans, and corn on top of the quinoa.
3. **Top with Dressing:** Add avocado dressing on top or pack separately.
4. **Serve:** Mix ingredients before eating for a balanced and nutritious lunch.

4. Fruit and Yogurt Parfait

Ingredients:

- 1/2 cup vanilla yogurt
- 1/4 cup granola
- 1/4 cup fresh strawberries, sliced
- 1/4 cup blueberries
- 1 tablespoon honey

Instructions:

1. **Layer Yogurt:** Start with vanilla yogurt at the bottom of the jar.
2. **Add Fruit:** Layer strawberries and blueberries on top of the yogurt.
3. **Add Granola:** Sprinkle granola over the fruit.
4. **Drizzle with Honey:** Add a drizzle of honey for extra sweetness.
5. **Serve:** Enjoy immediately or store in the refrigerator until lunchtime.

5. Pasta Salad Jars

Ingredients:

- 1/2 cup cooked pasta (such as penne or rotini)
- 1/4 cup cherry tomatoes, halved
- 1/4 cup diced cucumber
- 1/4 cup black olives, sliced
- 1/4 cup cubed mozzarella cheese
- 2 tablespoons Italian dressing

Instructions:

1. **Layer Dressing:** Start with Italian dressing at the bottom of the jar.
2. **Add Pasta:** Layer cooked pasta on top of the dressing.
3. **Add Veggies and Cheese:** Add cherry tomatoes, diced cucumber, black olives, and cubed mozzarella cheese.
4. **Serve:** Shake the jar to mix before eating, or pack the dressing separately.

6. Mini Sandwich Jars

Ingredients:

- 2 slices whole grain bread, cut into small squares
- 2 tablespoons cream cheese
- 1/4 cup sliced turkey or ham
- 1/4 cup sliced cucumber
- 1/4 cup shredded lettuce

Instructions:

1. **Prepare Sandwiches:** Spread cream cheese on bread squares, then layer with turkey or ham, cucumber slices, and shredded lettuce.
2. **Layer in Jar:** Place mini sandwiches in the jar.
3. **Serve:** Enjoy as a fun and easy-to-eat lunch option.

Tips for Perfect School Lunch Jars

- **Variety:** Incorporate a mix of proteins, grains, and vegetables to keep lunches interesting and balanced.
- **Portion Control:** Use jars of appropriate sizes to control portion sizes and prevent overeating.
- **Freshness:** Pack jars tightly to maintain freshness and prevent ingredients from mixing prematurely.
- **Creative Presentation:** Use colorful ingredients and fun shapes to make lunches more appealing to kids.

Nutritional Benefits

School lunch jars often include a variety of nutrient-dense ingredients, providing balanced meal with proteins, healthy fats, and essential vitamins and minerals. By incorporating fruits, vegetables, and whole grains, these jars support healthy growth and development while making mealtime enjoyable.

Conclusion

School lunch jars offer a practical and creative solution for busy families looking to provide nutritious and appealing meals for their children. With a variety of recipes that cater to different tastes and preferences, these jarred lunches make it easy to ensure kids are eating well while simplifying meal preparation. Enjoy the convenience and fun of jarred school lunches that mak lunchtime a delight.

Chapter 7:

Fitness and Wellness Jars 7.1.

Fitness and Wellness Jars 7.1

Introduction

Fitness and wellness are integral to maintaining a healthy lifestyle, and what you eat plays a crucial role in achieving your fitness goals. Fitness and wellness jars are designed to provide balanced nutrition that supports energy levels, aids in recovery, and promotes overall well-being. These jarred recipes are convenient for pre- or post-workout meals, snacks, or daily nutrition. Packed with protein, healthy fats, fiber, and essential vitamins, these jars are perfect for those who are active, health-conscious, or simply looking to improve their diet. This chapter explores various fitness and wellness jar recipes that are not only nutritious but also delicious and easy to prepare.

Basic Fitness and Wellness Jar Preparation

Ingredients:

- Lean proteins (such as chicken, tofu, or Greek yogurt)
- Whole grains (like quinoa, brown rice, or oats)
- Fresh vegetables and fruits
- Healthy fats (such as avocados, nuts, or seeds)
- Superfoods (like chia seeds, flaxseeds, or berries)
- Flavorful dressings or sauces

Instructions:

1. **Prepare Ingredients:** Cook grains, proteins, and any other components as needed. Chop vegetables and fruits.
2. **Layer Ingredients:** Begin with hearty ingredients like grains or proteins, followed by vegetables, fruits, and any additional toppings or dressings.
3. **Seal and Store:** Store jars in the refrigerator and ensure they are sealed tightly to keep ingredients fresh.

Fitness and Wellness Jar Recipes

1. Protein-Packed Quinoa Salad

Ingredients:

- 1/2 cup cooked quinoa
- 1/4 cup chickpeas, rinsed
- 1/4 cup diced cucumbers
- 1/4 cup cherry tomatoes, halved
- 1/4 cup crumbled feta cheese
- 2 tablespoons lemon-tahini dressing

Instructions:

1. **Layer Ingredients:** Start with quinoa at the bottom of the jar.
2. **Add Protein and Veggies:** Layer chickpeas, diced cucumbers, cherry tomatoes, and crumbled feta cheese.
3. **Top with Dressing:** Add lemon-tahini dressing on top or pack separately.
4. **Serve:** Shake the jar to mix before eating or enjoy as-is.

2. Greek Yogurt and Berry Smoothie Jars

Ingredients:

- 1/2 cup Greek yogurt
- 1/4 cup fresh strawberries, sliced
- 1/4 cup blueberries
- 1/4 cup raspberries
- 1 tablespoon chia seeds
- 1 tablespoon honey (optional)

Instructions:

1. **Layer Ingredients:** Start with Greek yogurt at the bottom of the jar.
2. **Add Berries:** Layer strawberries, blueberries, and raspberries on top of the yogurt.
3. **Add Chia Seeds:** Sprinkle chia seeds over the berries.
4. **Drizzle with Honey:** Add a drizzle of honey if desired.
5. **Serve:** Enjoy immediately or refrigerate for up to 2 days. Stir before eating for a creamy texture.

3. Sweet Potato and Black Bean Power Bowl

Ingredients:

- 1/2 cup roasted sweet potato cubes
- 1/4 cup black beans, rinsed
- 1/4 cup corn kernels
- 1/4 avocado, sliced
- 2 tablespoons salsa

Instructions:

1. **Layer Ingredients:** Start with roasted sweet potato cubes at the bottom of the jar.
2. **Add Beans and Veggies:** Layer black beans, corn kernels, and avocado slices.
3. **Top with Salsa:** Add salsa on top or pack separately.
4. **Serve:** Enjoy immediately or refrigerate until ready to eat.

4. Nut and Seed Energy Jars

Ingredients:

- 1/4 cup almonds
- 1/4 cup walnuts
- 1/4 cup pumpkin seeds
- 1/4 cup dried cranberries
- 1/4 cup dark chocolate chips

Instructions:

1. **Combine Ingredients:** Mix almonds, walnuts, pumpkin seeds, dried cranberries, and dark chocolate chips in a bowl.
2. **Fill Jars:** Spoon the mixture into jars.
3. **Serve:** Perfect as a quick snack or post-workout energy boost.

5. Avocado and Egg Breakfast Jars

Ingredients:

- 1/2 avocado, sliced
- 1 hard-boiled egg, sliced
- 1/4 cup cherry tomatoes, halved
- 1/4 cup spinach leaves
- 1 tablespoon balsamic vinaigrette

Instructions:

1. **Layer Ingredients:** Start with spinach leaves at the bottom of the jar.
2. **Add Veggies and Protein:** Layer cherry tomatoes, sliced avocado, and sliced hard-boiled egg.
3. **Top with Dressing:** Add balsamic vinaigrette on top or pack separately.
4. **Serve:** Enjoy immediately or store in the refrigerator for up to 2 days.

6. Chia Seed Pudding with Fresh Fruit

Ingredients:

- 1/4 cup chia seeds
- 1 cup almond milk (or any milk of choice)
- 1 tablespoon maple syrup
- 1/2 cup diced mango
- 1/2 cup strawberries, sliced

Instructions:

1. **Prepare Pudding:** In a bowl, mix chia seeds, almond milk, and maple syrup. Let sit for at least 30 minutes, or overnight, to thicken.
2. **Layer in Jar:** Spoon chia pudding into the jar.
3. **Add Fruit:** Top with diced mango and sliced strawberries.
4. **Serve:** Enjoy immediately or refrigerate for up to 3 days.

Tips for Perfect Fitness and Wellness Jars

- **Prepping Ahead:** Prepare jars in advance for quick grab-and-go meals or snacks.
- **Balance:** Ensure a good balance of proteins, healthy fats, and carbohydrates to support energy and recovery.
- **Freshness:** Use airtight jars to keep ingredients fresh and prevent spoilage.
- **Customization:** Adjust ingredients based on dietary preferences or fitness goals.

Nutritional Benefits

Fitness and wellness jars are designed to support an active lifestyle by providing essential nutrients that aid in energy production, muscle recovery, and overall health. Incorporating a mix of proteins, healthy fats, whole grains, and fresh produce ensures that you get a balanced intake of nutrients needed for optimal performance and well-being.

Conclusion

Fitness and wellness jars are a convenient and effective way to fuel your body with nutritious and balanced meals or snacks. By incorporating a variety of wholesome ingredients, these jars support your fitness goals and overall health. Enjoy the ease of preparing and storing these jars, and make the most of your active lifestyle with delicious and nutritious options that fit your needs.

High-Protein Meals 7.2.

Introduction

High-protein meals are essential for maintaining muscle mass, supporting recovery, and promoting satiety. Incorporating protein-rich foods into your diet can enhance your overall wellness and aid in meeting fitness goals. Whether you're looking for a hearty lunch, a satisfying dinner, or a powerful post-workout meal, high-protein jars offer a convenient and nutritious solution. This chapter features a collection of high-protein jar recipes designed to be both delicious and easy to prepare, ensuring you get the protein your body needs to perform at its best.

Basic High-Protein Jar Preparation

Ingredients:

- Lean proteins (such as chicken, turkey, tofu, or beans)
- Dairy or dairy alternatives (like Greek yogurt, cottage cheese, or almond milk)
- Whole grains (like quinoa, brown rice, or farro)
- Fresh vegetables
- Healthy fats (such as avocado or nuts)
- Flavorful dressings or sauces

Instructions:

1. **Prepare Ingredients:** Cook proteins, grains, and any other components as needed. Chop vegetables and prepare dressings or sauces.
2. **Layer Ingredients:** Start with proteins or grains at the bottom of the jar, followed by vegetables, and any additional toppings or dressings.
3. **Seal and Store:** Seal jars tightly and store in the refrigerator. Enjoy your high-protein meal within a few days for optimal freshness.

High-Protein Jar Recipes

1. Chicken and Quinoa Power Bowl

Ingredients:

- 1/2 cup cooked quinoa
- 1/2 cup grilled chicken breast, sliced
- 1/4 cup black beans, rinsed
- 1/4 cup corn kernels
- 1/4 cup diced red bell peppers
- 2 tablespoons avocado dressing

Instructions:

1. **Layer Ingredients:** Start with quinoa at the bottom of the jar.
2. **Add Chicken:** Layer sliced grilled chicken breast on top of the quinoa.
3. **Add Beans and Veggies:** Add black beans, corn kernels, and diced red bell peppers.
4. **Top with Dressing:** Add avocado dressing on top or pack separately.
5. **Serve:** Mix the jar contents before eating or enjoy as-is.

2. Greek Yogurt and Berry Protein Parfait

Ingredients:

- 1/2 cup Greek yogurt
- 1/4 cup mixed berries (such as strawberries, blueberries, and raspberries)
- 1/4 cup granola
- 1 tablespoon chia seeds
- 1 tablespoon honey (optional)

Instructions:

1. **Layer Yogurt:** Start with Greek yogurt at the bottom of the jar.
2. **Add Berries:** Layer mixed berries on top of the yogurt.
3. **Add Granola and Chia Seeds:** Sprinkle granola and chia seeds over the berries.
4. **Drizzle with Honey:** Add a drizzle of honey if desired.
5. **Serve:** Enjoy immediately or refrigerate for up to 2 days. Stir before eating.

3. Turkey and Veggie Stir-Fry Jars

Ingredients:

- 1/2 cup cooked brown rice
- 1/2 cup ground turkey, cooked
- 1/4 cup sliced bell peppers
- 1/4 cup broccoli florets
- 1/4 cup snap peas
- 2 tablespoons teriyaki sauce

Instructions:

1. **Layer Rice:** Start with cooked brown rice at the bottom of the jar.
2. **Add Turkey:** Layer cooked ground turkey on top of the rice.
3. **Add Veggies:** Layer sliced bell peppers, broccoli florets, and snap peas.
4. **Top with Sauce:** Add teriyaki sauce on top or pack separately.
5. **Serve:** Shake the jar to mix ingredients before eating or heat for a warm meal.

4. Tofu and Vegetable Stir-Fry

Ingredients:

- 1/2 cup cooked quinoa
- 1/2 cup tofu, cubed and sautéed
- 1/4 cup sliced carrots
- 1/4 cup snap peas
- 1/4 cup bell peppers, diced
- 2 tablespoons soy sauce or tamari

Instructions:

1. **Layer Quinoa:** Start with cooked quinoa at the bottom of the jar.
2. **Add Tofu:** Layer sautéed tofu on top of the quinoa.
3. **Add Veggies:** Add sliced carrots, snap peas, and diced bell peppers.
4. **Top with Sauce:** Add soy sauce or tamari on top or pack separately.
5. **Serve:** Mix before eating or heat if desired.

5. Salmon and Avocado Rice Bowl

Ingredients:

- 1/2 cup cooked brown rice
- 1/2 cup cooked salmon, flaked

- 1/4 avocado, sliced
- 1/4 cup cucumber, diced
- 1/4 cup shredded carrots
- 2 tablespoons lemon-tahini dressing

Instructions:

1. **Layer Rice:** Start with cooked brown rice at the bottom of the jar.
2. **Add Salmon:** Layer flaked salmon on top of the rice.
3. **Add Veggies:** Add sliced avocado, diced cucumber, and shredded carrots.
4. **Top with Dressing:** Add lemon-tahini dressing on top or pack separately.
5. **Serve:** Enjoy immediately or refrigerate until ready to eat.

6. Cottage Cheese and Fruit Jar

Ingredients:

- 1/2 cup cottage cheese
- 1/4 cup pineapple chunks
- 1/4 cup sliced strawberries
- 1 tablespoon chia seeds
- 1 tablespoon chopped walnuts

Instructions:

1. **Layer Cottage Cheese:** Start with cottage cheese at the bottom of the jar.
2. **Add Fruit:** Layer pineapple chunks and sliced strawberries on top of the cottage cheese.
3. **Add Chia Seeds and Walnuts:** Sprinkle chia seeds and chopped walnuts over the fruit.
4. **Serve:** Enjoy immediately or store in the refrigerator for up to 2 days.

Tips for Perfect High-Protein Jars

- **Protein Variety:** Incorporate different protein sources like lean meats, dairy, legumes, and tofu to keep meals interesting.
- **Freshness:** Use airtight jars to maintain freshness and prevent spoilage.
- **Balanced Meals:** Ensure each jar includes a balance of proteins, grains, and vegetables for a well-rounded meal.
- **Preparation:** Prepping jars in advance can save time and ensure you have healthy options readily available.

Nutritional Benefits

High-protein jars support muscle growth, repair, and recovery, making them ideal for active individuals. Protein helps to maintain satiety, reducing the likelihood of snacking on less nutritious foods. By including a variety of protein sources along with other essential nutrients, these jars contribute to overall health and well-being.

Conclusion

High-protein meals in jars are a practical and delicious way to support your fitness and wellness goals. With a range of recipes that cater to different tastes and preferences, these jars offer convenience and nutrition in one. Enjoy the ease of preparing and storing high-protein meals, and make the most of your active lifestyle with flavorful, protein-packed options.

Post-Workout Snacks 7.3.

Introduction

After an intense workout, your body needs to replenish energy stores, repair muscle tissue, and support recovery. Post-workout snacks are crucial for providing the right balance of protein, carbohydrates, and healthy fats to aid in these processes. Jars are an excellent way to prepare and store these snacks, making them convenient and easy to grab after exercise. This chapter offers a variety of post-workout jar recipes designed to optimize recovery, boost energy levels, and satisfy hunger.

Basic Post-Workout Jar Preparation

Ingredients:

- Protein sources (such as Greek yogurt, cottage cheese, protein powder, or lean meats)
- Carbohydrate sources (like fruits, whole grains, or sweet potatoes)
- Healthy fats (such as nuts, seeds, or avocado)
- Hydrating components (like coconut water or fresh fruits)
- Flavor enhancers (such as honey, cinnamon, or vanilla extract)

Instructions:

1. **Prepare Ingredients:** Cook and chop ingredients as needed. Prepare protein sources, grains, and any sauces or flavorings.
2. **Layer Ingredients:** Start with the main protein source, followed by carbohydrates, healthy fats, and any additional components.
3. **Seal and Store:** Use airtight jars to keep snacks fresh and store them in the refrigerator. Enjoy within a few days for optimal freshness.

Post-Workout Snack Jar Recipes

1. Greek Yogurt and Berry Recovery Jar

Ingredients:

- 1/2 cup Greek yogurt

- 1/4 cup fresh strawberries, sliced
- 1/4 cup blueberries
- 1/4 cup granola
- 1 tablespoon honey

Instructions:

1. **Layer Yogurt:** Start with Greek yogurt at the bottom of the jar.
2. **Add Berries:** Layer fresh strawberries and blueberries on top of the yogurt.
3. **Add Granola:** Sprinkle granola over the berries.
4. **Drizzle with Honey:** Add a drizzle of honey for extra sweetness.
5. **Serve:** Enjoy immediately or refrigerate for up to 2 days. Stir before eating for a creamy texture.

2. Cottage Cheese and Pineapple Bowl

Ingredients:

- 1/2 cup cottage cheese
- 1/4 cup pineapple chunks
- 1 tablespoon chia seeds
- 1 tablespoon chopped almonds

Instructions:

1. **Layer Cottage Cheese:** Start with cottage cheese at the bottom of the jar.
2. **Add Pineapple:** Layer pineapple chunks on top of the cottage cheese.
3. **Add Chia Seeds and Almonds:** Sprinkle chia seeds and chopped almonds over the pineapple.
4. **Serve:** Enjoy immediately or store in the refrigerator for up to 2 days.

3. Protein-Packed Smoothie Jar

Ingredients:

- 1 cup almond milk (or any milk of choice)
- 1 scoop protein powder (vanilla or chocolate)
- 1/2 banana, sliced
- 1/4 cup spinach leaves
- 1 tablespoon peanut butter

Instructions:

1. **Blend Ingredients:** In a blender, combine almond milk, protein powder, banana, spinach leaves, and peanut butter.
2. **Pour into Jar:** Pour the smoothie mixture into a jar.
3. **Serve:** Enjoy immediately or store in the refrigerator for up to 1 day. Shake well before drinking.

4. Sweet Potato and Black Bean Snack

Ingredients:

- 1/2 cup roasted sweet potato cubes
- 1/4 cup black beans, rinsed
- 1/4 cup diced bell peppers
- 1/4 avocado, diced
- 2 tablespoons salsa

Instructions:

1. **Layer Sweet Potato:** Start with roasted sweet potato cubes at the bottom of the jar.
2. **Add Beans and Veggies:** Layer black beans, diced bell peppers, and diced avocado.
3. **Top with Salsa:** Add salsa on top or pack separately.
4. **Serve:** Enjoy immediately or store in the refrigerator for up to 2 days.

5. Chocolate Chia Seed Pudding

Ingredients:

- 1/4 cup chia seeds
- 1 cup almond milk (or any milk of choice)
- 1 tablespoon cocoa powder
- 1 tablespoon maple syrup
- 1/4 cup fresh raspberries

Instructions:

1. **Prepare Pudding:** In a bowl, mix chia seeds, almond milk, cocoa powder, and maple syrup. Let sit for at least 30 minutes, or overnight, to thicken.
2. **Layer in Jar:** Spoon chia pudding into the jar.
3. **Add Raspberries:** Top with fresh raspberries.
4. **Serve:** Enjoy immediately or refrigerate for up to 3 days.

6. Almond Butter and Apple Slices

Ingredients:

- 1/4 cup almond butter
- 1 apple, sliced
- 1 tablespoon granola (optional)

Instructions:

1. **Layer Almond Butter:** Start with almond butter at the bottom of the jar.
2. **Add Apple Slices:** Layer apple slices on top of the almond butter.
3. **Add Granola (Optional):** Sprinkle granola on top if desired.
4. **Serve:** Enjoy immediately or pack apple slices separately to prevent browning.

Tips for Perfect Post-Workout Jars

- **Timing:** Consume your post-workout snack within 30-60 minutes after exercise for optimal recovery.
- **Portion Control:** Adjust portion sizes based on your specific energy and nutritional needs.

- **Freshness:** Use airtight jars to keep snacks fresh and prevent spoilage.
- **Variety:** Rotate recipes to keep post-workout snacks interesting and balanced.

Nutritional Benefits

Post-workout snacks are designed to provide a mix of proteins, carbohydrates, and healthy fats, essential for muscle repair, replenishing energy stores, and reducing muscle soreness. Including ingredients like Greek yogurt, cottage cheese, and sweet potatoes ensures you're getting the right nutrients to support recovery and performance.

Conclusion

Post-workout snacks in jars offer a convenient and nutritious way to aid in recovery and replenish energy. With a variety of recipes that cater to different tastes and preferences, these jars make it easy to support your fitness goals and maintain overall health. Enjoy the practicality and deliciousness of post-workout jars as part of your wellness routine.

Detox Jars

Introduction

Incorporating detox-friendly foods into your diet can help your body eliminate toxins, boost your energy levels, and promote overall wellness. Detox jars are designed to support your body's natural cleansing processes while providing essential nutrients and flavors. This chapter features a variety of detox jar recipes that are not only refreshing and nourishing but also easy to prepare. These jars are perfect for those looking to give their system a gentle reset or simply enjoy clean, healthy meals.

Basic Detox Jar Preparation

Ingredients:

- Fresh fruits and vegetables (such as leafy greens, cucumbers, and berries)
- Detoxifying herbs and spices (like ginger, turmeric, and mint)
- Hydrating ingredients (coconut water, lemon juice)
- Whole grains (quinoa, brown rice)
- Lean proteins (tofu, chicken, or legumes)

Instructions:

1. **Prepare Ingredients:** Wash and chop fruits and vegetables. Cook grains and proteins if needed. Prepare any herbs or spices.
2. **Layer Ingredients:** Start with hearty ingredients like grains or proteins, followed by vegetables, fruits, and any additional herbs or dressings.

3. **Seal and Store:** Use airtight jars to maintain freshness and store them in the refrigerator. Consume within a few days for the best results.

Detox Jar Recipes

1. Green Detox Smoothie Jar

Ingredients:

- 1 cup spinach leaves
- 1/2 cucumber, peeled and sliced
- 1/2 green apple, cored and sliced
- 1/2 lemon, juiced
- 1 tablespoon chia seeds
- 1 cup coconut water

Instructions:

1. **Layer Ingredients:** Start with spinach leaves at the bottom of the jar.
2. **Add Cucumber and Apple:** Layer sliced cucumber and green apple on top.
3. **Add Lemon Juice and Chia Seeds:** Drizzle lemon juice and sprinkle chia seeds over the top.
4. **Pour Coconut Water:** Add coconut water, or pack separately if preferred.
5. **Serve:** Blend before drinking or enjoy as a refreshing, hydrating jarred snack.

2. Detox Veggie and Quinoa Salad

Ingredients:

- 1/2 cup cooked quinoa
- 1/4 cup shredded carrots
- 1/4 cup diced bell peppers (red, yellow, or orange)
- 1/4 cup chopped celery
- 1/4 cup chickpeas, rinsed
- 2 tablespoons lemon-tahini dressing

Instructions:

1. **Layer Quinoa:** Start with cooked quinoa at the bottom of the jar.
2. **Add Veggies and Chickpeas:** Layer shredded carrots, diced bell peppers, chopped celery, and chickpeas on top.
3. **Top with Dressing:** Add lemon-tahini dressing or pack separately.
4. **Serve:** Mix before eating or enjoy as a crisp and refreshing salad.

3. Berry and Chia Seed Detox Pudding

Ingredients:

- 1/4 cup chia seeds
- 1 cup almond milk (or any milk of choice)

- 1 tablespoon maple syrup
- 1/2 cup mixed berries (such as strawberries, blueberries, and raspberries)
- 1 teaspoon grated ginger

Instructions:

1. **Prepare Pudding:** In a bowl, mix chia seeds, almond milk, and maple syrup. Let sit for at least 30 minutes or overnight to thicken.
2. **Layer in Jar:** Spoon chia pudding into the jar.
3. **Add Berries:** Top with mixed berries and grated ginger.
4. **Serve:** Enjoy immediately or refrigerate for up to 3 days.

4. Turmeric and Avocado Detox Bowl

Ingredients:

- 1/2 cup cooked brown rice
- 1/4 avocado, sliced
- 1/4 cup cherry tomatoes, halved
- 1/4 cup shredded cabbage
- 1/4 cup cooked chickpeas
- 1/2 teaspoon turmeric powder
- 2 tablespoons lemon-ginger dressing

Instructions:

1. **Layer Rice:** Start with cooked brown rice at the bottom of the jar.
2. **Add Toppings:** Layer sliced avocado, cherry tomatoes, shredded cabbage, and cooked chickpeas.
3. **Season with Turmeric:** Sprinkle turmeric powder over the top.
4. **Add Dressing:** Drizzle lemon-ginger dressing on top or pack separately.
5. **Serve:** Enjoy as a nutritious and detoxifying meal.

5. Cucumber and Mint Infused Water Jar

Ingredients:

- 1/2 cucumber, thinly sliced
- 1/4 cup fresh mint leaves
- 1 lemon, sliced
- 1 liter water

Instructions:

1. **Combine Ingredients:** In a large jar, combine cucumber slices, mint leaves, and lemon slices.
2. **Add Water:** Pour water over the ingredients.
3. **Infuse:** Let the mixture infuse in the refrigerator for at least 2 hours or overnight.
4. **Serve:** Enjoy as a refreshing detox drink throughout the day.

6. Sweet Potato and Kale Detox Bowl

Ingredients:

- 1/2 cup roasted sweet potato cubes
- 1/2 cup kale, chopped
- 1/4 cup quinoa
- 1/4 cup pomegranate seeds
- 2 tablespoons apple cider vinegar dressing

Instructions:

1. **Layer Quinoa:** Start with cooked quinoa at the bottom of the jar.
2. **Add Sweet Potato and Kale:** Layer roasted sweet potato cubes and chopped kale on top.
3. **Add Pomegranate Seeds:** Sprinkle pomegranate seeds over the kale.
4. **Top with Dressing:** Drizzle apple cider vinegar dressing on top or pack separately.
5. **Serve:** Mix before eating or enjoy as a vibrant and detoxifying meal.

Tips for Perfect Detox Jars

- **Hydration:** Include hydrating ingredients like coconut water or cucumber to support detoxification.
- **Freshness:** Use airtight jars to keep ingredients fresh and prevent spoilage.
- **Variety:** Rotate different detox recipes to keep your diet interesting and nutritionally balanced.
- **Preparation:** Prepping jars ahead of time can save you effort and ensure you always have a healthy detox option on hand.

Nutritional Benefits

Detox jars are designed to support the body's natural cleansing processes by including ingredients known for their detoxifying properties. These recipes focus on providing hydration, fiber, antioxidants, and essential nutrients to help the body eliminate toxins, boost energy, and promote overall well-being.

Conclusion

Detox jars offer a convenient and delicious way to support your body's natural detoxification process. With a variety of refreshing and nourishing recipes, these jars make it easy to incorporate detox-friendly foods into your routine. Enjoy the benefits of enhanced wellness and vitality with these vibrant and healthful jarred options.

As we wrap up our journey through the diverse and delicious world of jarred meals, it's clear that preparing and enjoying meals in a jar offers not just convenience but also a pathway to healthier, more balanced eating. From breakfast to dinner, snacks to desserts, and even special dietary needs, these jarred recipes provide a versatile and practical solution for anyone looking to streamline their meal prep while embracing a variety of flavors and nutritional benefits.

Embracing the Convenience

The primary advantage of meals in a jar is their convenience. Whether you're a busy professional, a student juggling multiple responsibilities, or someone who simply enjoys having meals readily available, these jarred recipes allow you to prepare and store your meals in advance. The airtight seal of a jar ensures freshness, making it easier to maintain a healthy eating routine amidst a hectic lifestyle.

Nutritional Diversity and Balance

Our exploration of meals in a jar has shown that these recipes can cater to various dietary preferences and needs. From high-protein options to detox-friendly meals, low-carb choices, and vegan delights, the versatility of jarred meals means that you can tailor your diet to support your health goals. By incorporating a wide range of ingredients—from lean proteins and whole grains to fresh vegetables and nutritious fats—these jars ensure that you receive a balanced mix of nutrients with every meal.

Practical Tips for Success

Throughout the book, we've shared practical tips for preparing and storing meals in jars to maintain their freshness and flavor. Remember to:

- **Prepare Ahead:** Take advantage of batch cooking and prepping to make your meals more convenient and time-efficient.
- **Layer Wisely:** Proper layering helps maintain the texture and flavor of ingredients, ensuring that your meals are as enjoyable as they are nutritious.
- **Use Airtight Jars:** To keep your meals fresh and prevent spoilage, invest in high-quality airtight jars.
- **Get Creative:** Don't be afraid to experiment with different ingredients and flavors to keep your meals exciting and satisfying.

The Joy of Meal Prep

Embracing meal prep with jars not only simplifies your cooking process but also empowers you to take control of your dietary choices. By dedicating a little time to preparing your meals in advance, you can enjoy the benefits of nutritious, homemade food every day. The recipes in this book are designed to inspire and motivate you to explore new culinary possibilities and make your meal prep enjoyable.

Looking Ahead

As you continue to use and adapt the recipes in **Meals in a Jar**, we hope you find joy in the creativity and simplicity of jarred meals. Whether you're looking for quick snacks, hearty lunches, or indulgent desserts, there's a jarred option for every taste and need. The principles of meal prep, balance, and convenience will serve you well as you navigate your journey towards healthier eating and a more organized lifestyle.

Thank you for joining us on this culinary adventure. We encourage you to keep exploring, experimenting, and enjoying the wonderful world of meals in a jar. Here's to delicious, nutritious, and convenient eating!

Made in United States
Troutdale, OR
11/20/2024